The following endorsements were written for the original 1991 edition. The contemporary titles of each endorser has been maintained, while each individual's current position (if applicable) is indicated in parentheses.

"David Dockery's *Doctrine of the Bible* represents Southern Baptist scholarship at its best. The volume is timely, conservative, and helpful. Written in an easy-to-understand style, it helps folks in the pew, pastors, teachers alike to frame a satisfactory concept of the Divine Word of God. What a pleasure to commend these pages."
 – *Darold H. Morgan (1924-2019), president emeritus, Annuity Board of the Southern Baptist Convention*

"*The Doctrine of the Bible* is a stalwart restatement of scriptural authority and a trustworthy guide through the critical issues of revelation, inspiration, and the total truthfulness of the Bible. The volume is thoroughly evangelical, pleasantly readable, and will be tremendously useful for individuals, churches, and study groups. Dockery has established a solid reputation for his insightful and faithful treatment of these issues, and Baptists stand in his debt for this helpful contribution."
 – *R. Albert Mohler Jr., editor, The Christian Index (now president, The Southern Baptist Theological Seminary)*

"David Dockery has brought together the different facets of the doctrines of the Bible (revelation, the relation of the Testaments, self-testimony, the divine and the human, inspiration, truthfulness, text, canon, interpretation, authority) into a confessed and coherent whole. Many Christians can be helped to understand more clearly how our Bible came to be and how it ought to be read, studied, pondered, and obeyed today, especially within the life and worship of the church. One does not necessarily have to agree with all of the author's conclusions (for example, the 'plenary' theory of inspiration, or the 'balanced inerrancy' view) to make constructive use of this timely book.
 – *James Leo Garrett Jr. (1925–2020), professor of theology, The Southwestern Baptist Theological Seminary*

"*The Doctrine of the Bible* is *must* reading for Southern Baptists who are seeking a way 'beyond the impasse' regarding the Bible. David Dockery is a trusted and proven scholar who transcends polemics and emotion in this comprehensive yet readable book. His work is excellent. I do not know of any writing which could be more meaningful if Southern Baptists really want to come together on the Bible. I hope it has wide acceptance."

– John P. Newport (1917-2000), vice president for academic affairs and provost (retired), distinguished professor of philosophy of religion emeritus, The Southwestern Baptist Theological Seminary

"If for no other reason than its fair and judicious treatment of issues which have troubled the Southern Baptist Convention for at least the last three decades, David S. Dockery's *The Doctrine of the Bible* deserves widespread reading among Southern Baptists of all political and theological varieties. But the value of this work extends far beyond the current controversy in Southern Baptist life. David Dockery's work is in fact such a fair and balanced treatment of the doctrines of biblical inspiration and authority that it should find a wide readership in American Christianity.

The great value of this piece lies in its ability to raise, synthesize, and reflect upon the breadth of biblical and theological questions surrounding the doctrine of inspiration. In this connection, Dockery's book serves the whole church, for it requires those of a more traditional view of inspiration to reflect honestly upon the questions that trouble their less traditional fellow Christians; and it requires the less traditional to see that a wholesale rejection of historic doctrines of biblical inspiration and authority may in fact likewise be too facile an act. Dockery's book is herewith warmly commended. It is clear without being simplistic; it is scholarly without being tedious; and it is thoroughly evangelical without being tendentious. Its humility of tone serves well the confession that Dockery so evidently espouses."

– Robert B. Sloan, George Truett Professor of Religion, Baylor University (now president, Houston Baptist University)

"Serious Bible students will quickly recognize *The Doctrine of the Bible* by David S. Dockery as a watershed in Southern Baptist publications on the nature of divine revelation and the Bible as God's Word. The book is significant for the seriousness of its content, the quality of its scholarship, and the scope of its perspective on the Bible. The writer communicates with clarity, investigates his subject comprehensively, and affirms the uniqueness and authority of the Bible with persuasion. The book clarifies theological emphases reflected by current leadership in the Southern Baptist Convention. The publication demands thoughtful consideration by the serious reader and explains numerous aspects of the Bible related to a decade of Southern Baptist discussion on the nature and authority of the Bible."
— *Roy L. Honeycutt (1926-2004), president, The Southern Baptist Theological Seminary*

"A superb statement of the historic Baptist doctrine of Holy Scripture, masterfully written and clearly presented. This study will serve the renewal of the church by helping us to listen afresh to God's inspired Word. Never before have we needed this emphasis more urgently than today. I recommend this book to every pastor and every congregation."
— *Timothy George, dean, Beeson Divinity School, Samford University (now research professor of divinity, Beeson Divinity School)*

"David Dockery has written a book on the Bible and what it says about itself that should be required reading for every Southern Baptist as well as every Christian. Dockery has combined brilliant scholarship with a deep-felt, reverential faith to produce a comprehensive, yet very readable volume—no easy task. He deserves an enthusiastic, 'Well done!'"
— *Richard D. Land, executive director, Christian Life Commission of the Southern Baptist Convention (now president, Southern Evangelical Seminary)*

"David Dockery is a master teacher. In his book *The Doctrine of the*

Bible, he has transformed complex theological terms of the seminary classroom into the practical language of the pew. Against the backdrop of the last decade within our beloved convention he clearly answers questions about the Bible which many Southern Baptists have been asking. I encourage every Southern Baptist to read this book. It will become a ready resource about the precious Word of God for years to come."

> *– Morris H. Chapman, president, Southern Baptist Convention; pastor, First Baptist Church, Wichita Falls, Texas (now president emeritus, Executive Committee of the Southern Baptist Convention)*

"Since Baptists are people of the Book, we must fully understand and appreciate the perfect treasure that is the written Word of God. David Dockery made a tremendous contribution toward that end when he first released *The Doctrine of the Bible* nearly 30 years ago. The passage of time has not diminished the relevance and importance of the topic of Scripture's nature and authority, so I am delighted that Seminary Hill Press is making available to a new generation of Southern Baptists this critical work by an alumnus and now distinguished faculty member of Southwestern Seminary. The duty of maintaining fidelity to our heritage as a people of the Book is a perennial task, and Dr. Dockery's volume is an invaluable resource and guide for pastors and church members in this noble calling."

> *-- Adam W. Greenway, president, The Southwestern Baptist Theological Seminary*

"Nearly three decades ago, I recommended this important book as 'a stalwart restatement of scriptural authority and a trustworthy guide through the issues of revelation, inspiration, and the total truthfulness of the Bible.' I stand by that statement. But now, I also want to underline the fact that this book made history in the Southern Baptist Convention. *The Doctrine of the Bible* is a powerful restatement of the evangelical Scripture principle, and it arrived just when we needed it. Now, well into the 21st century, we need it again, and I am so pleased by this new edition. David Dockery is one of the most significant theologians and intellects in the evangelical world, and this book is needed now, more than ever."

> *-- R. Albert Mohler Jr., president, The Southern Baptist Theological Seminary*

"David Dockery's *The Doctrine of the Bible* was, and is, a remarkable combination of erudition and simplicity. When one knows a subject as well as Dr. Dockery does, it is often difficult to refine it down to easily digestible, yet very informative chapters. Albert Einstein is reported to have said, 'If you can't explain it simply, you don't understand it well enough.' Clearly, Dr. Dockery understands the doctrine of the Bible, and when you read this book, you will too!"

    -- Richard Land, president, Southern Evangelical Seminary

"In a day when faithfulness to Scripture is waning, David Dockery, a great theologian and Southern Baptist educator, provides a thorough explanation and defense of biblical doctrine in *The Doctrine of the Bible*. His clear, concise communication and easy-to-read prose make this salient work accessible to the serious Bible student as well as to a layperson. This timeless work is saturated in Scripture and gives its readers the resources necessary to fight against the fiery darts of doubt, confusion, and irreverence. This book is an essential tool for believers who value the authenticity of Scripture and who unyieldingly embrace the necessity of Bible doctrine."

    -- Robert Smith Jr., Charles T. Carter Baptist Chair of Divinity,
       Beeson Divinity School, Samford University

"About the time the first release of David Dockery's *The Doctrine of the Bible* hit the shelf, I was sitting in his classroom at Southern Seminary. I had already witnessed, firsthand, why Southern Baptists so desperately needed not only the book, but why we needed scholars like David Dockery. On a unified affirmation of the truthfulness of Scripture, Southern Baptists and their seminaries have come a long way since then. But the Bible, from which all our doctrine is derived, is, in many ways, the core doctrine. Another release of the book that helped shore up our denomination's understanding of that core doctrine is a worthy endeavor ... in every generation."

    -- Paul Chitwood, president, International Mission Board

"One can hardly overstate the importance of the doctrine of Scripture. Yet, perhaps no other doctrine is at once so consistently affirmed in belief but persistently neglected in study. With theological precision and pedagogical skill, Dr. Dockery presents in *The Doctrine of the Bible* a theology of the Bible that is both erudite and accessible, nuanced and clear. Eminently relevant, this book clings without compromise to that which is theologically essential, but also confronts without cowering that which is culturally harmful. Indeed, in this author's own words, 'a renewed commitment to the truthfulness and dependability of Scripture is the first step toward healing the deadly sickness in today's theological trends.' May a new generation of Baptists hear—and heed—the words of this revered and faithful scholar."

> -- *Katie J. McCoy, assistant professor of theology in women's studies, Scarborough College*

THE DOCTRINE OF THE

BIBLE

DAVID S. DOCKERY

SEMINARY HILL
═══ PRESS ═══

The Doctrine of the Bible
By David S. Dockery
Copyright © 2020 by Seminary Hill Press

Seminary Hill Press (SHP) is the publishing arm of The Southwestern
Baptist Theological Seminary, 2001 West Seminary Drive, Fort Worth,
Texas 76115.

Previously published by Convention Press, 1991.

Unless otherwise noted, all Scripture quotations are from the Christian
Standard Bible®, Copyright © 2017 by Holman Bible Publishers. Used by
permission. Christian Standard Bible® and CSB® are federally registered
trademarks of Holman Bible Publishers.

Scripture quotations marked KJV are from the King James Version,
public domain.

Hardback
ISBN-13: 978-1-7327740-4-9

Paperback
ISBN-13: 978-1-7327740-5-6

To my parents,
Sam and Pansye Dockery,
who from the days of my childhood taught me
"the sacred Scriptures, which are able
to give you wisdom for salvation
through faith in Christ Jesus"
(2 Timothy 3:15).

Table of Contents

Preface to the 1991 Edition

Baptists are a people of the Book. The Book is the Bible. This book is a book about the Bible, God's written Word to His people. It has been a special privilege to write this book at this time in Baptist life, especially in light of the Sunday School Board's Centennial observance in 1990-91. Writing a book about the Bible has also been a huge responsibility, considering the current wide-ranging discussions about biblical inspiration, interpretation, and authority in the evangelical world. In light of these factors, I have written with the prayer that I might say something helpful and constructive to people during these important times.

This book could have been written a number of different ways. I did not attempt to survey every viewpoint on every subject discussed in each chapter. Entire books have been and could be written on each chapter's subject matter. I make no comprehensive claims for the book. However, I have attempted to provide a careful overview of the important themes related to a doctrine of Scripture. When I have considered it helpful, I have presented a variety of views, especially on matters of present concern in the broader Baptist and evangelical communities. Particularly, I have tried to offer representative approaches in areas such as inspiration, inerrancy, and interpretation. Each time, however, I have tried to reach a conclusion that could be supported by the biblical, theological, and historical materials.

As Basil Manly indicated in his preface to *The Doctrine of Inspiration*, "Originality on a subject like this, which has been under discussion for centuries, would surely be error."[1] My work does not have as its primary aim to be original or creative. The aims of this book, written more than a century after Manly's, are similar to his. He said: "There may be, after all, honest independence of inquiry, a careful sifting of opinions, a fair recasting of views in the mould of one's own thinking, and a subordination of the whole simply to the controlling authority of God's Word. This is all at which I have aimed."[2]

Similarly, I have tried to present material that is consistent with the tradition of most Southern Baptists, while always setting forth my own beliefs on each subject. That tradition is represented by James P. Boyce; John A. Broadus; Basil Manly, Jr.; A.T. Robertson; B.H. Carroll; J.M. Frost; and many more. Perhaps a quotation from Frost, the founding editor and first secretary of the Sunday School Board, would be appropriate in the Board's Centennial year: "We accept the Scriptures as an all-sufficient and infallible rule of faith and practice, and insist upon the absolute inerrancy and sole authority of the Word of God."[3] This book is written in that tradition about the Book, God's written Word.

The book is intended for people in the church. With this in mind, I have avoided technical discussions. When it has been important to use that standard language of the theological world, I have tried to define those words. The book's goal is to help people in the churches better understand the nature of the Bible so we can better understand and obey its message.

I have chosen to limit the number of notes, but I have included a bibliography at the end of the book. I hope that this approach will help readers pursue further study on this important subject.

During the project I have felt the strength of God and have sensed the prayers of His people. I am grateful to the Discipleship Training Department of the Sunday School Board for giving me this unique opportunity. This year has been a time of family transition. My move to the Sunday School Board has altered my writing schedule considerably; the editors, particularly Don Atkinson, have been patient with my tardiness. For their kindness and encouragement I am thankful. My family has been especially sensitive and supportive. To each member— Lanese, Jonathan, Benjamin, and Timothy—I express my love and deepest gratitude.

Several persons have offered valuable encouragement and suggestions in the process of planning and writing this book. I deeply appreciate each of them. Their encouragement and suggestions have been valuable, and the book is much improved because of their contributions.

It is my prayer that because of this book God's people will renew their confidence in Scripture and will be more willing to obey it. I have been reminded while writing this book of the heavy responsibility involved in such obedience. Thus, I pray the same for myself and my family. Together I trust we can sing with renewed commitment,

How firm a foundation, ye saints of the Lord,
Is laid for your faith in His excellent Word![4]

SOLA DEO GLORIA
David S. Dockery
Reformation Day 1990

Endnotes

[1]Basil Manly, *The Doctrine of Inspiration* (New York: Armstrong and Son, 1888), 5-6.

[2]Ibid., 6.

[3]J.M. Frost, *Baptist Why and Why Not* (Nashville: The Sunday School Board, 1900), 12.

[4]John Rippon, "How Firm a Foundation."

Preface to the 2020 Edition

It seems nearly impossible to imagine that it has been almost 30 years since the initial publication of *The Doctrine of the Bible*. I remember working on key aspects of the book as if it were yesterday. The preface for the book's first edition was completed in the fall of 1990. Now, the book is being re-released in the spring of 2020 as an aspect of the "Baptists and the Bible" conference on the campus of The Southwestern Baptist Theological Seminary. I am deeply grateful to President Adam W. Greenway for his kind invitation to circulate the book once again as a Seminary Hill Press publication.

The initial volume was written during some tense years of the "inerrancy controversy" in Southern Baptist life. This book was originally written as the text for the SBC's annual doctrine study. It was written at a time when there were many questions being raised about the nature of Holy Scripture and the meaning of words like *inspiration*, *infallibility*, and *inerrancy*. While the big questions related to these themes have been answered and settled at this time both for convention leaders and for the large majority of those who serve across the SBC, some of the same questions that were at the forefront three decades ago continue to linger for some pastors and laypeople in the churches.

Moreover, if one takes a step back and looks at the landscape across other sectors of the larger Christian community and the culture at-large, concerns related to the truthfulness and authority of Scripture loom large in a context that seems more and more to be shaped by the influences of secularization, pluralization, and privatization. People wrestle with the idea of truth, meaning, and purpose, as well as issues of life, sexuality, and moral order. The number of people without any religious affiliation continues to rise. This trend is especially evident among those who are under 35 years old. While these trends do not necessarily point to a rise of atheism or agnosticism, they do point to a spirituality that is disconnected from Holy Scripture, from the church, and from Christian doctrinal foundations.

These trends underscore what the late Peter Berger (1929-2017), former scholar in the fields of sociology and culture, called *cognitive contamination*, leading to the loss of plausibility structures. The loss of plausibility structures regarding the truthfulness of Holy Scripture and the transformational power of the Gospel seems now to make it much easier for each succeeding generation in North America to dismiss the claims of the Bible or to ignore them altogether.

Perhaps in God's good providence, this little book may provide encouragement for some to reexamine the message of Scripture and there re-discover the drama of the redemptive message found only in Jesus Christ. We pray that the book will serve as a guide for others who have questions about the Bible, its meaning, and its authority. Primarily, we hope that the book will strengthen the convictions of God's faithful people, granting them assurance of the full truthfulness and complete authority of God's Word written as the inward work of God's Spirit bears witness by and with the Word in our hearts.

We believe the book represents the best of the Baptist tradition represented by Benjamin Keach (1640-1704), Dan Taylor (1738-1816), Andrew Fuller (1754-1815), Francis Wayland (1796-1884), Alvah Hovey (1820-1903), Basil Manly, Jr. (1825-1892), Lottie Moon (1840-1912), B.H. Carroll (1843-1914), Charles Octavius Booth (1845-1924), J.M. Frost (1848-1916), Herschel Hobbs (1907-1995), W.A. Criswell (1909-2002), Carl F.H. Henry (1913-2003), and a host of other Baptist thinkers and leaders. Southern Baptists, with all of our struggles, squabbles, and shortcomings, remain a people committed to the Book. Indeed, Southern Baptists are a People of the Book.

It was a great privilege to be invited to write this book 30 years ago, and it is an honor to have it published once again by Seminary Hill Press. The text of the book is unchanged with the exception of minor changes to conform to SHP style, and minor corrections, additions, and clarifications to reflect significant developments since 1991, including an updated bibliography. The biblical references have been changed from the text of the NIV to that of the CSB. The original endorsements for the book are included to remind everyone of the Southern Baptist context in which the book was written three decades ago. We trust this little book will still serve as a helpful tool for some in our current Baptist context as well.

I am grateful to the entire Seminary Hill Press team, led by James A. Smith Sr., who labored faithfully to make this a reality, including Alex Sibley, Emil Handke, Harold Apples, Caitlyn Jameson, Katie Coleman, and Julie Owens. I also express my gratitude to LifeWay Christian Resources for permitting Seminary Hill Press to reprint the volume.

I am grateful for my wife, Lanese, our sons and daughters-in-law, as well as our grandchildren, who have offered support and encouragement for this project and for many other writing opportunities through the years. Their faithful prayers mean more than I can express. We trust the Lord will use the book for good in the lives of His people in the days and years to come.

SOLA DEO GLORIA
David S. Dockery
Distinguished Professor of Theology
The Southwestern Baptist Theological Seminary
New Year's Day 2020

CHAPTER 1

Revelation and the Bible

Word Alert

Revelation—an uncovering, a removal of the veil, a disclosure of what was previously unknown, God's manifestation of Himself to humankind in such a way that men and women can know and have fellowship with Him.

General revelation—God's self-disclosure in a general way to all people at all times in all places. God reveals Himself through nature, history, our experience, and our conscience.

Particular revelation—God's self-manifestation in a particular way to particular people at particular times and places.

Personal revelation—revelation viewed primarily as a personal experience or encounter with God in Christ. It focuses attention on the dynamic and personal characteristics of God's manifestation of Himself to men and women.

Propositional revelation—God's self-manifestation understood as information about God, including the divine interpretation of revelatory events. A proper view of Christian truth distinguishes between the personal and propositional aspects but does not separate them.

All knowledge of God comes by way of revelation. The knowledge of God is revealed knowledge, since it is God who gives it. He bridges the gap between Himself and His creatures and discloses Himself and His will to them. God is the source of knowledge about Himself, His ways, and His truth. By God alone can God be known. The knowledge of God is revealed by His self-manifestation.

In a famous essay on revelation, Archbishop William Temple exclaimed:

> The dominant problem of contemporary religious thought is the problem of revelation. Is there such a thing at all? If there is, what is its mode and form? Is it discoverable in all existing things, or only in some? If in some, then in which, and by what principle are these selected as its vehicle? Where is it found, or believed to be found, what is its authority?[1]

Although these questions were posed over 80 years ago, they still remain striking issues in our day. We cannot address each question comprehensively. In this opening chapter we will focus on God's self-revelation, that is, His manifestation of Himself and His will. We will make a distinction between general and special revelation. We will emphasize Jesus Christ as God's final revelation. Finally, we will focus on the Bible as the source of God's revelation for today's believers.

Revelation: God's Self-Disclosure

The word *revelation* means *an uncovering, a removal of the veil, a disclosure of what was previously unknown.* More specifically, revelation is God's manifestation of Himself to humankind in such a way that men and women can know and have fellowship with Him. An example of revelation is found in the biblical narrative in which Simon Peter declares that Jesus is the Christ, the Son of God (see Matthew 16:16). Jesus responded to this declaration, "Blessed are you, Simon son of Jonah, because flesh and blood did not reveal this to you, but my Father in heaven" (Matthew 16:17). That Jesus is the Son of God could be known only through revelation. The veil was removed; the gap in the disciples' knowledge was bridged. God the Father revealed Himself to the disciples, and they perceived the knowledge of Jesus as His Son. The knowledge of Jesus' sonship was not attained by human discovery, nor could it have been; it came from God alone.

All Christians recognize that God has revealed Himself to His creatures by acting and speaking in history. Yet opinions vary about what constitutes revelation. Is there a natural or general revelation? Is special revelation rational or meaningful? Let us turn our attention to these matters.

General Revelation

It would be a misconception to think of physical nature as a part of God in the same way that my hand is a part of me. Yet God might reveal Himself through His actions as a person often does. Let us consider how this might occur. Besides speaking or writing, persons may reveal facts about themselves in other ways, such as physical gestures or facial expressions. Sometimes persons' actions communicate whether they are selfish or generous, clumsy or skillful. A grimace, a smile, or a frown can often be revealing. Transferring this idea to a theological context is not simple, because God is not visible. He does not have facial features or body parts with which to gesture. Nature is not identical with God or even part of God. When we say that God reveals Himself through nature, we mean that through the events of the physical world God communicates to us things about Himself that we would otherwise not know.

What sort of things might God tell us in this manner? In Romans 1:19-20, Paul wrote that "what can be known about God is evident among them, because God has shown it to them. For his invisible attributes, that is, his eternal power and divine nature, have been clearly seen since the creation of the world, being understood through what he has made. As a result, people are without excuse."[2] This point echoes an affirmation the psalmist made centuries earlier: "The heavens declare the glory of God" (Psalm 19:1). The psalmist saw the glory of God through general revelation, though his communication of his observations, inspired by God's Spirit, became special revelation to his readers. But it is very important to note that what the psalmist saw was objectively and genuinely there. In other words, all that can be known about God in a *natural* sense has been revealed in nature. This is called natural or general revelation.[3] General revelation is universal in the sense that it is *God's self-disclosure of Himself in a general way to all people at all times in all places.* General revelation occurs through nature, through human experiences and conscience, and through history. We will consider each of these avenues of general revelation.

Wonders of nature. God manifests Himself in the wonders of the heavens—sun, moon, and stars—and in the beauty of the earth—skies and seas, mountains and forests, grass and flowers. Whether in the smallest atom or the largest galaxy, the simplest form of life or the most complex, God reveals Himself through His works. As Jesus maintained, God "causes his sun to rise on the evil and the good, and sends rain on the righteous and the unrighteous" (Matthew 5:45), thus revealing His goodness to all. Likewise, Luke recorded that "the living God, who made the heaven, the earth, the sea, and everything in them … did not leave himself without a witness, since He did what is good by giving you rain from heaven and fruitful seasons and filling you with food and your hearts with joy" (Acts 14:15-17). God makes Himself known in the continuing care and provision for humankind. The universe as a whole serves the Creator's purpose as a vehicle for God's self-manifestation.

Experience of humans. God also reveals Himself in men and women, who are made in the image and likeness of God (see Genesis 1:26-27). Humans, as a direct creation of God, mirror and reflect God. People are God's unique workmanship. This uniqueness is evidenced by humans' dominion over the rest of creation; in the capacity people possess to reason, feel, and imagine; in humans' freedom to act and respond; and in humans' sense of right and wrong (see Genesis 1:28; Romans 2:14-15). Especially through this moral sense God reveals Himself in the consciences of men and women. The fact that religious belief and practice are universal confirms the apostle's statements in Romans 2. Yet the creatures who worship; pray; build temples, idols, and shrines; and seek God in diverse ways do not glorify God as God or give Him thanks (see Romans 1:21-23). Nevertheless, because persons have been given the capacity for receiving God's general revelation, they are responsible for the way they respond to it.

Workings of history. The combined experience of humans makes up history, another source of God's general revelation. God manifests Himself in the workings of history. All of history, rightly understood, bears the imprint of God's activity and thus has a theological character. Primarily, God is revealed in history through the rise and fall of peoples and nations. The history of nations reflects some manifestation of God at work.

Paul on Mars Hill asserted that God has made Himself known in history and that He is no unknown God. Rather, He is the true God who commands all people everywhere to repent (see Acts 17:22-31).

Inadequate for salvation. God's general revelation is plain, whether in nature, in human conscience, or in history. Even though it is plain, it is often misinterpreted because sinful and finite humans are trying to understand a perfect and infinite God.

What we have seen so far is compatible with the following:

1. Religious belief is a nearly universal human phenomenon.
2. Such religious belief is implanted by God.
3. All people ought to acknowledge God on the basis of what they learn from the world around them.
4. All people probably believe in the existence of God, even though some do not admit it.[4]

No one, no matter how seemingly insignificant or limited, can be excused for missing God's revelation. Enough knowledge of God is revealed in a flower to lead a child or a scientist to acknowledge God and worship Him. Sufficient evidence lies in a tree, a fingerprint, a snowflake, or a grain of sand to cause us to glorify the true God. But people *will not* do this. Instead, they substitute nature, parts of nature, or their own experience for God and find their hearts darkened.

The light of nature is not sufficient to impart the knowledge of God necessary for salvation. The revelation of God through nature reveals His power (see Romans 1:20), goodness (see Matthew 5:45), and righteousness (see Romans 2:14-15); but it does not reveal His saving grace. This grace is revealed only through special revelation. The revealed will of God, His special revelation, is necessary for men and women to know how to worship Him rightly. A manifestation of God is in His general revelation, but human sinfulness perverts the reception of this manifestation. General revelation is plain enough to leave all people without excuse before God; nevertheless, it does not succeed in bringing people to a saving knowledge of God. It is as if a lawyer were offered the information necessary to solve a case yet perversely chose to ignore it. Although the information by itself would not solve the case, if diligently followed, it would. The purpose of God's revelation is to promote the worship of Himself. The results of the perversity of sin leave men and women without excuse.

In summary, men and women lack the willingness to come to a pure and clear knowledge of God. They have no excuse, because the fault of rejection lies within the human heart. It is impossible to pretend to be ignorant of God's revelation. Human conscience itself convicts humankind of rejection and ingratitude. Men and women suppress God's truth because they do not like the truth about God. They do not like the God to whom the truth leads them; so instead, they invent substitute gods and religions. The universal presence of religion on earth is evidence of this substitution. God has revealed Himself to all people at all times in all places; thus, people everywhere express a need for God. This expression may be found in sophisticated laws of culture, in materialism, in the gods and goddesses of world religions, or in the bestial images of paganism. These expressions support the fact that human beings throughout history have consistently and willfully rejected God because they will not respond to God. Therefore, they need something or someone else to take God's place (see Romans 1:18-32). According to Paul, our suppressing the awareness of God and His demands warps our reason and conscience. Because we reject God, He righteously reveals His wrath against humankind. Although God's general revelation does not bring one into a saving relationship with God, it reveals God to His creatures; therefore, they are responsible for their responses.

Special Revelation

We have learned that God has revealed Himself in nature, human experience, and history. But sin's entrance into the world has changed the revelation, as well as the interpretation of it. What is needed to understand God's self-disclosure fully is His special revelation. Indeed, as noted in our discussion of Psalm 19, special revelation provides the viewpoint through which we can fully understand and appreciate God's revelation. Divine truth exists outside special revelation; but it is consistent with and supplemental to, not a substitute for, special revelation. General revelation is consistent with special revelation yet distinct from it.[5]

Particular revelation. In contrast to God's general revelation, which is available to all people, *God's special revelation is available to specific people at specific times in specific places.* This revelation is available now only by consultation of sacred Scripture. Special revelation is, first of all, particular. God reveals Himself to His people. These people of God are the children of Abraham, whether by natural (see Genesis 12:1-3) or spiritual descent (see Galatians 3:16, 29). Does this mean that God confines knowledge of Himself to a particular people? Not necessarily, because God's general revelation has been given to all, though perverted and rejected by the universal wickedness of humankind. He now chooses to whom and through whom He will make Himself known. As with Abraham, God said, "All the peoples on earth will be blessed through you" (Genesis 12:3). This is God's purpose in manifesting Himself in a particular manner to His people: that they will be a channel of blessing to others.

Progressive revelation. Special revelation is also progressive. In the witness of biblical history is found a developing disclosure of God, His will, and His truth in the Old and New Testaments. The development is not contradictory in any fashion. It is complementary and supplementary to what had been previously revealed. We should think of the progress not from untruth to truth but from a lesser to a fuller revelation (see Hebrews 1:1-3). The revelation of the law in the Old Testament is not superseded by the Gospel but is fulfilled in it. The latter fulfills the former.

Personal revelation. In recognition of the human predicament God chose from the very beginning to disclose Himself in a direct way. God has entered this world throughout the course of history. He has made Himself known to us within time and space. God has acted and spoken to redeem the human race from its own self-imposed evil. Through miracles, the exodus, and ultimately Jesus Christ, God has revealed Himself in history. Special revelation includes not only those acts in history but also the prophetic-apostolic interpretations of those events.

Special revelation is primarily redemptive and personal. God revealed Himself personally as "I AM" (Exodus 3:14). He talked to Moses face-to-face as with a friend (see Exodus 33:11). Like His appearance to Samuel (see 1 Samuel 3:21), His many personal encounters continued in the covenants and throughout the Old Testament.

The ultimate point of God's personal revelation is found in Jesus Christ. In Him the Word became flesh (see John 1:1, 14; 14:9). God was decisively confronting people in Jesus Christ. The good tidings that the holy and merciful God promises salvation as a divine gift to people who cannot save themselves has been fulfilled in the gift of His Son. The redemptive revelation of God is that the incarnate Word (Jesus Christ) has borne the sins of fallen humanity, has died in its place, and has been raised to ensure justification. This is the fixed center of special revelation.

Propositional revelation. Likewise, God's self-disclosure is propositional in that it made known truths about Him to His people. This assertion has been rejected by much modern theology. But it certainly seems plausible that knowledge *about* someone precedes intimate knowledge *of* someone. The primary purpose of revelation is not necessarily to enlarge the scope of one's knowledge about God. Yet the purpose of knowledge about God is coming to know God.

We can thus affirm that special revelation has three stages. The first is redemption in history. This ultimately centers in the work of the Lord Jesus Christ. The second is the written source of God's revelation, the Bible. In Holy Scripture God has provided interpretive records of what He has done for the redemption of men and women. The third is the work of the Holy Spirit in the lives of individuals and in the corporate life of the church. The Spirit applies God's revelation to the minds and hearts of His people, sometimes distinguished as illumination. As a result, men and women receive Jesus Christ as Lord and Savior and are enabled to follow Him faithfully in a believing, covenant community until life's end.

The content of special revelation is primarily God Himself. Revelation involves removing the veil, bridging the gap so that God makes Himself known in His self-manifestation. Mystery remains in God's self-revelation. God does not fully reveal Himself to any person. No person could fully understand; and beyond that, the full manifestation of God would result in the death of the recipient (see Exodus 33:20). However, God reveals Himself to persons to the degree they can receive it.

Not only is the mystery of God Himself unveiled, but God's truth is also revealed. Special revelation is the declaration of truth about God, His character, and His actions and relationship with His creation. His self-disclosure is intelligible and meaningful, communicating divine truth for the mind and heart. The purpose of God's gracious manifestations was well stated by the apostle Paul: "He made known to us the mystery of his will, according to his good pleasure that he purposed in Christ as a plan for the right time—to bring everything together in Christ, both things in heaven and things on earth in him" (Ephesians 1:9-10).

The proper setting of special revelation is Christian faith. God makes Himself known to those who receive His revelation in faith. Faith is the instrument by which we receive God's revelation. When faith is present, the things of God become manifest (see Hebrews 11:1, 6).

Faith is the glad recognition of truth, the reception of God's revelation without reservation or hesitation (see Romans 10:17). God is pleased to reveal Himself and His majestic Word to people of faith.

Revelation: The Witness of Scripture

Today it is evident that the Bible is of crucial importance, for it is through the Bible that the Spirit witnesses to individuals of God's grace and the need for a response of faith. In the Bible we learn of God's redemption of sinners in Christ Jesus. Our response of faith to God's words and acts, recorded and interpreted by the prophets and the apostles, calls for us to embrace with humble teachableness, without finding fault, whatever is taught in Holy Scripture.

God has initiated the revelation of Himself to men and women. This revelation is understandable to humankind, making it possible to know God and to grow in relationship with Him. God's self-manifestation provides information about Himself for the purpose of leading men and women into God's presence. For believers today the Bible is the source of God's revelation. In the written Word we can identify God; know and understand something about Him, His will, and His work; and point others to Him. Special revelation is not generally speculative. The Bible primarily speaks on matters of cosmology and history when these issues touch the nature of faith. God has manifested Himself incarnationally through human language, human thought, and human action as ultimately demonstrated in the incarnation of Jesus Christ. Since the person and work of Jesus Christ are the fixed center of special revelation, we will move to a discussion of Jesus Christ and the Bible. But first it will be helpful to provide an overview of the Bible, including its names, contents, and characteristics.

Names of the Bible

The English word *Bible* is derived from the Greek word *biblion* or *biblia*, which means *scroll(s)* or *book(s)*. English-speaking Christians use three major titles to refer to this holy Book. We call it the Bible, the Scripture or Scriptures, and the Word of God. These words, as we use them today, have a far more significant connotation than the Greek word *biblion*. *Biblion* was a roll of papyrus, a reed-like plant, whose inner bark was dried and fashioned into a writing material widely used in the ancient world. *Biblion* could be used to designate books of magic (see Acts 19:19) or a bill of divorce (see Mark 10:4), as well as sacred books. To believers the word *Bible* refers to the Book par excellence, the recognized source of divine revelation for contemporary believers.

In Daniel 9:2 the Greek translation used *ta biblia* to refer to the prophetic writings. Paul used the word *biblia* when he wrote to Timothy and asked him to bring the books (see 2 Timothy 4:13), by which he probably referred to some scrolls containing the Hebrew Scriptures, which we usually call the Old Testament. This usage passed into the postapostolic church (see 2 Clement 14:2). Sometime during this period a significant change occurred in the common usage of the plural *biblia* to the singular *biblion*. This change reflected the growing conception of the Bible as one utterance of God rather than as a multitude of voices speaking for Him.

Even before the canonization of the sacred books (see chapter 7), importance was attached to the sacred writings. Moses wrote "all the words of the Lord" in the "covenant scroll" (Exodus 21-23; 24:4-7). Joshua's farewell address was written "in the book of the law of God" (Joshua 24:26). Samuel spoke words about the manner of the kingdom and "wrote them on a scroll, which he placed in the presence of the Lord" (1 Samuel 10:25). Jesus repeatedly appealed to the authoritative Scriptures (see Matthew 19:4; 22:29). Similarly, Paul and the apostles thought of the scrolls as "the very words of God" (Romans 3:2).

The term *Scripture* is a rendering of the Greek word *graphe*. The plural form identifies the whole collection of sacred writings (see Matthew 21:42; 1 Corinthians 15:3-4). The singular form can mean either a specific passage (see Mark 12:10) or the constituent body of writings (see Galatians 3:22). Paul characteristically used *gramma* (*writing* or *Scripture*) to refer to the Torah or the law. In 2 Timothy 3:15 he referred to the "sacred Scriptures" (*hiera grammata*), which Timothy had known since he was a child and which were able to make him wise for salvation.

The divine author of Scripture is the Holy Spirit (see Acts 28:25), who has breathed out Scripture as a function of His creative activity. This sacred Book's instruction is divine and authoritative for salvation and for Christian living.

Christian theology appeals to the authority of Scripture because it sees Scripture as the written Word of God. Since the time of the Second London Confession (1677) Baptists have not hesitated to use the term "Word of God written."[6] However, this identification of Scripture with the Word of God has been called into question in recent times. Some contend that the Bible merely contains the word of God and then only insofar as it becomes the "word of God for me" to the individual soul. To regard the Bible in its full extent as the Word of God written would be to claim that it was composed by the superintending work of the Holy Spirit. It is this action of the Spirit, however, over the work of biblical writers that the apostles themselves claimed (see 2 Timothy 3:16; 2 Peter 1:19-21) and that requires the characterization "Word of God" for the sacred writings.

It is very important to recognize that the designation *Word of God* or *Word of the Lord* is appropriately used in three distinct contexts. Primarily, the phrase refers to (1) Jesus Christ. The phrase rightly points to (2) the divinely disclosed message through God's spokesmen and this in principle to (3) the biblical writings. The three usages are certainly related, lying within one another in concentric circles. So the phrase belongs to Christ, the ultimate, total Word; to the proclamation of Christ in the apostolic church; and to the truth of Christ embodied in written form in the Scriptures.

This concept of Scripture specifies the prophetic declarations from God to and through His servants (see Numbers 3:16, 51; Joshua 19:50; 22:9; 2 Samuel 22:31; Proverbs 30:5; Isaiah 5:24) and numerous occasions in Psalms (see Psalm 119:11, 105). The New Testament appears to use the terms *Word of God, Word of the Lord, Word of Jesus,* and *Word of Christ* with similar, almost synonymous and interchangeable meanings. The Word of God, which was at first orally proclaimed, was finally embodied in written form in the New Testament.

Our Lord authenticated this usage by declaring that Scripture as the Word of God cannot be broken (see John 10:35). It is "the prophetic word strongly confirmed" about which the apostle wrote, because these words were spoken from God as the writers "were carried along by the Holy Spirit" (2 Peter 1:19-21). It is biblically and theologically right to acknowledge that the prophetic-apostolic word is God's Word written. Without the writing there would be no Bible, no Scriptures, and therefore no Word of God available to us. The Bible is God's Word written.

The Bible itself does not indicate what title we should use. Therefore, we can use *the Bible, the Scriptures,* or *the Word of God* interchangeably in our study.

Characteristics of the Bible

The Bible has two major parts that we commonly call the Old Testament and the New Testament. What the Jewish people call the Hebrew Scriptures, Christians generally refer to as the Old Testament. The origin of these terms is related to the Bible's covenant themes.

God made a covenant with Abraham (see Genesis 12:1-3) in which He promised to bless Abraham and to make Abraham a blessing. God promised the people of Israel that they would be "my kingdom of priests and my holy nation" (Exodus 19:6). Similarly, God said, "I will walk among you and be your God, and you will be my people" (Leviticus 26:12). The promises of Abraham were ratified with Isaac and Jacob and reaffirmed with Abraham's descendants through Moses after the Exodus. The covenant promises were expanded with David (see 2 Samuel 7). After the division of the kingdom, following Solomon's reign, and the conquering of the northern and the southern kingdoms by Assyria and Babylon, many people thought that God had forsaken His covenant people. The prophet Jeremiah, however, proclaimed that God would make a new covenant with the nation (see Jeremiah 31:31-34). God's dealing with people in anticipation of the coming of Christ is the major theme of the 39 Old Testament books.

The term *new covenant* appears several times in the New Testament.

Jesus used it when He instituted the Lord's Supper (see Luke 22:20). With this usage Jesus sought to call attention to the new basis of fellowship with God established by Jesus' death. The apostle Paul also spoke of that new covenant (see 1 Corinthians 11:25; 2 Corinthians 2:14-3:18), as did the author of Hebrews (see Hebrews 8:7-13; 9:11-15; 10:15-18). The description of God's dealings with people on the basis of the new covenant is the major theme of the 27 New Testament books.

There was no Old Testament or New Testament before the coming of Christ, only one collection of sacred writings. But after the apostles produced another body of sacred literature, the church began to distinguish between the two. The covenant identified God's unalterable promise of the spiritual blessing and guidance of His people. Among the church fathers the Latin term *testamentum* was used to translate *covenant*, and from there the term passed into English. So the old and new covenants became the Old and New Testaments.

The Old Testament was written in Hebrew, though a few chapters were written in a similar language, Aramaic. Customarily, the Jewish people divided the Old Testament into three large sections called the Law, the Prophets, and the Writings (Luke 24:44). Sometimes only two distinctions were employed, the Law and the Prophets. Christians arrange the Old Testament into four groups: the Law or Pentateuch (Genesis through Deuteronomy); the Historical books (Joshua through Esther); the Poetic/Wisdom books (Job through the Song of Solomon); and the Prophets (Isaiah through Malachi), divided into Major and Minor Prophets (Major referring to books that are long and Minor to books that are relatively short).

If one adopts the view that Moses wrote the first five books of the Old Testament (the position adopted in the Old and New Testaments, including the words of Jesus), the earliest Old Testament books were probably written between 1400 and 1200 B.C. If the final writing was Malachi (ca. 400 B.C.), then the 39 books were composed over a period of about 1,000 years. Probably all the writers were Jews and included prophets, judges, kings, and other leaders in Israel.

The New Testament was written in Greek, though Jesus and His disciples apparently spoke Aramaic. A few Aramaic words were scattered throughout the New Testament. The 27 books, as we have them in our Bible, follow a generally logical arrangement. They begin with the four books called Gospels (Matthew through John) that describe the birth, death, and resurrection of Christ. The Book of Acts begins where the four Gospels end, describing the birth of the church and the advancement of the Christian mission. Acts introduces the apostle Paul and his church-planting efforts. Following Acts we find a group of letters. The first group of letters (13) consists of writings from Paul to churches and young ministers, arranged from the longest to the shortest. Following the Pauline Letters are a group of letters called Catholic Letters or General Letters. The last book, Revelation, is an apocalyptic work.

The New Testament was written during a 50-year period. There is some question whether James, Galatians, or 1 Thessalonians was written first. It is generally agreed that Revelation was composed last in the waning years of the first century. All the writers were Jews, with the exception of Luke, who wrote the Gospel of Luke and Acts (though some think that Luke was also a Jew). The writers represent a variety of occupations, including fishers, doctors, tax collectors, and religious leaders.

Together the Old and New Testaments consist of 66 books. Many of these writings were not originally designed as books, in the sense of being written for publication and public distribution. Several (like Philemon) were private documents, and others (2 and 3 John) were too short to be called books. But all of them have been collected and now are published in one Book, the Bible. It is appropriate, therefore, to refer to these books as the Bible.

In addition to the major sections identified above (Law, Prophets, Poetry, Gospels, and Epistles or Letters), several other types of literature in the Bible are referred to as literary genres, or types. These include poems, parables, hymns, narratives, creeds, sermons, and apocalypses.

In spite of the diversity of authors, languages, genres, and composition, spanning almost 1,500 years, the Bible has a remarkable unity. The unity is the result of the one divine Author's superintending the production of many human authors to present the divine message to humankind.

Conclusion

The Bible presents a message about God and His purposes. It describes the creation of the universe, including the direct creation of men and women in a paradise on earth. The Bible describes the call of Abraham, the giving of the law, the establishment of the kingdom, the division of the kingdom, and the captivity and restoration of Israel. Scripture sees humankind as fallen from a sinless condition and separated from God. The promise of a coming Messiah who will redeem men and women and reign as King appears throughout the Old Testament.

The message of the Word of God proclaims that believers are restored to favor with God through the sacrifice of Christ. His sacrifice put an end to the Old Testament sacrificial system in which the blood of animals represented the handling of the sin problem. The New Testament reveals the Christ who brought salvation and describes how these prophecies about Him were minutely fulfilled. This unifying message ties the biblical library together. The Old Testament promises were fulfilled in the person of Jesus Christ, "the Son of Abraham" and "the Son of David" (Matthew 1:1). As Augustine said more than 1,500 years ago, "The New is in the Old contained; the Old is in the New explained." This overarching unity centers in Jesus Christ. It is to the subject of Jesus Christ and the Bible that we now turn.

Endnotes

[1] William Temple, in *Revelation*, ed. John Baille and Hugh Martin (New York: MacMillan Publishing Co., 1937), 83.

[2] It should be noted that commentators differ over the meaning of Paul's message. Who are these Gentiles? Was this true only before or during Paul's day? Is this observation universally applicable? Those questions are beyond our discussion but are nevertheless pertinent.

[3] An affirmation of natural revelation is not an affirmation of natural

theology, though we believe that there is a theology of nature. See G.C. Berkower, *General Revelation* (Grand Rapids: William B. Eerdmans Publishing Co., 1955), 117-136.

[4]Paul Helm, *Divine Revelation: The Basic Issues* (Westchester: Crossway Books, 1982), 6.

[5]Portions of the information in this chapter can be found in David S. Dockery, "The Doctrine of Revelation and Inspiration," *Indiana Baptist*, 18 October 1988, 4-5.

[6]William L. Lumpkin, *Baptist Confessions of Faith* (Valley Forge: The Judson Press, 1959), 249.

CHAPTER 2

Jesus Christ and the Bible

Word Alert

Christology—the study of the teaching of Christ, His person, and His nature. In earlier times Christology also included the work of Christ, now usually considered under the doctrine of salvation (soteriology).

Christology from below—used in this chapter to emphasize that the study of Jesus Christ should begin with His human nature and earthly life.

Christology from above—used in this chapter to suggest that the study of Jesus Christ should begin with His divine nature and heavenly preexistence.

Arians—followers of the teaching of Arius, an elder in Alexandria (A.D. 318-325). Basically, Arianism taught that God the Father alone is God. This belief contended that God could not possibly have communicated His essence to any other. Thus, the Son (Jesus) was a created being. Arianism was declared heretical at both the Council of Nicea (A.D. 325) and the Council of Constantinople (A.D. 381).

Docetists—a group in the early church who regarded the human nature of Christ and His sufferings as imaginary rather than part of a real incarnation.

Ebionites—an early Christian sect that accepted Jesus as the prophetic successor to Moses but denied His deity and preexistence.

Jesus Christ is the central figure of the New Testament and the focus of the Christian faith. The New Testament is our primary source of information about Jesus. Yet the New Testament's testimony is amply supported by the impact of Jesus Christ on the world of the first century. Our concern in this chapter is to recognize the importance of Jesus' view of the Old Testament, His authentication of the New Testament, and His authority as a teacher. We will also look briefly at a matter that will receive further attention in chapter 4: the significance of Jesus as divine-human in regard to the divine-human aspect of Scripture.

Jesus Christ: The Promised Messiah

Jesus was born in Bethlehem of Judea, a few miles south of Jerusalem. He was born a Jew. In different ways and at various times God had spoken to His people through His prophets (see Hebrews 1:1). The purposes of God had been made known through a series of covenants (see Genesis 12; 2 Samuel 7; Jeremiah 31). In these covenants God's intent for establishing His kingdom and for redeeming humankind is progressively expressed. God's purposes were to be accomplished through a descendant of David. The people of God in the Old Testament looked forward expectantly to the coming of the promised King, their Messiah. In Jesus Christ these covenant promises found their ultimate fulfillment.

The Old Testament includes two different lines of teaching about the Promised One, sometimes distinct and other times commingled. One line claims that the Messiah would be a Redeemer who would restore humankind to a right relationship with God. This theme is best developed around the idea of a Suffering Servant Messiah in Isaiah 52:13-53:12. Here the Messiah is pictured as one who would become an offering for the sins of men and women.

Another line of Old Testament teaching describes the Messiah as a coming King destined to restore Israel to its rightful place as God's people on earth. The promises portray the restoration as a time of peace and righteousness.

Aspects of each purpose can be seen in the covenant promises and the prophetic pictures, though the details of the completion of these teachings remained somewhat unclear. The New Testament, however, interprets the Old Testament and announces that the promised Messiah has come in Jesus of Nazareth. Through His ministry, teachings, sacrificial death, and resurrection, Jesus fulfilled the messianic promises, accomplished the messianic mission, and provided for the salvation of a lost world. The New Testament also declares that Jesus will come again and will reign as King, bringing peace and joy and righteousness.

In identifying Jesus as the Messiah, the New Testament authors affirm an essential unity between the Old Testament and the New Testament. The New Testament, which is rooted in the Old Testament, interprets and amplifies the Old Testament. The life and work of Jesus, therefore, were founded in the Old Testament, which Jesus acknowledged to be the Word of God (see John 10:35) and on which He based His life.

Jesus Christ: Old Testament Scripture

The New Testament account of the ministry of Jesus maintains that Jesus Himself was responsible for teaching His followers that His life and ministry fulfilled the Scriptures. Jesus interpreted the Scriptures in a manner similar to contemporary Jewish exegetes, but His method and message were novel.

This new method was a Christological reading, which means that Jesus read the Old Testament in light of Himself. For example, in John 5:39 Jesus said: "You pore over the Scriptures because you think you have eternal life in them, and yet *they testify about me*" (emphasis added). In John 5:46 Jesus said, "For if you believed Moses, you would believe me, because *he wrote about me*" (emphasis added). Also, on the Emmaus road with His disciples following the resurrection, Jesus said: "'How slow [you are] to believe all that the prophets have spoken! Wasn't it necessary for the Messiah to suffer these things and enter into his glory?' Then beginning with Moses and all the Prophets, he interpreted for them the things concerning himself in all the Scriptures" (Luke 24:25-27).

In the temptation narratives (see Matthew 4:1-11; Luke 4:1-13), in which we find Jesus' own estimation of His status and calling, His answers were taken from Deuteronomy 6-8. In this passage Moses, following the 40 years of wandering in the wilderness, exhorted Israel to wholehearted obedience and continued faith in the divine provision for them. It was a time of hunger and testing, preparatory to a special task, in which God disciplined His nation Israel to teach it to worship only the true God (see Deuteronomy 8:5). Israel often failed to carry out the mission and call of God. Jesus, at the end of the 40 days, accepted afresh His messianic mission and His status as the Son of God. His belief in His forthcoming resurrection after three days seemed to be motivated both by the promises of Israel's resurrection (see Hosea 6:2) and by seeing the account of Jonah as a picture of His own resurrection (see Jonah 1:17; Matthew 12:40). He observed that His own experience prefigured in the psalms of vindication and suffering. These psalms were used both by the individual Israelites and by corporate Israel (see Psalm 22; 41-43; 118; Matthew 21:42; 23:39; 26:38; 27:46).[1]

R.T. France sums up the evidence in these words:

> He uses *persons* in the Old Testament as types of himself (David, Solomon, Elijah, Elisha, Isaiah, Jonah) or of John the Baptist (Elijah); he refers to Old Testament *institutions* as types of himself and his work (the priesthood and the covenant); he sees in the *experiences* of Israel foreshadowings of his own; he finds the hopes of Israel fulfilled in himself and his disciples and sees his disciples as assuming the *status* of Israel; in Israel's *deliverance* by God he sees a type of the gathering of men into his church, while the *disasters* of Israel are foreshadowings of the imminent punishment of those who reject him, whose *unbelief* is prefigured in that of the wicked in Israel and even, in two instances, in the arrogance of the Gentile nations.[2]

In all these aspects of the Old Testament people of God, Jesus saw foreshadowings of Himself and His work. The result was that Jesus was opposed and rejected by the majority of the Jews, while the true Israel was now to be found in the new Christian community. The history of Israel had reached its decisive point in the coming of Jesus. The whole of the Old Testament was summed up in Him. He embodied in Himself the redemptive destiny of Israel. That status and destiny are to be fulfilled in the community of those who belong to Him.

Because Jesus is the fulfillment of God's purpose for Israel, words originally spoken of the nation can rightly be applied to Him. Likewise, because Jesus is the representative of humankind, words spoken originally by the psalmist can be fulfilled (see John 13:18; 15:25; 19:28). Jesus is the key to understanding the Old Testament because everything points to Himself. The New Testament writers, following the pattern of Jesus, interpreted the Old Testament as a whole and in its parts as a witness to Christ.

The Gospels indicate that Jesus understood His mission in a way that ran counter to the assumptions and expectations of His closest followers, as well as of His opponents. One thing is for sure: Jesus saw His mission as a fulfillment of the Scriptures.[3] We can agree with C.K. Barrett's comment: "The gospel story as a whole differs so markedly from current [that is, first-century] interpretation of the Old Testament that it is impossible to believe that it originated simply in meditations on prophecy; it originated in the career of Jesus of Nazareth."[4]

It is not surprising that in providing different pictures of Jesus' life, the biblical writers saw that at almost every point He had fulfilled the Old Testament. This realization provides the key to the way Jesus understood and used the Old Testament. It also lays the groundwork for Jesus' authentication of the New Testament.

Jesus Christ: The Apostolic Witness

In the Gospels we learn that Jesus understood His own life in light of the Scriptures. We learn, too, that He accepted the full authority and divine authorship of the Old Testament and that He claimed truth for His own teaching. We know that the New Testament was written after Jesus' life on earth. What, then, was His relationship to the New Testament?

During His ministry on earth Jesus trained disciples. Among these, 12 were given special intimacy (see Mark 3:14). It is impossible to speak with certainty about the methods Christ used to teach His disciples. Probably, however, Jesus instructed His followers by methods similar to the rabbis of His day. Fifteen times in the Gospels He is called Rabbi. At other times He is referred to as Teacher or Lord, which are vitally related ideas. The rabbis thought of themselves as bearers of truth or of the true tradition. It was their task to pass on truth to approved disciples, who memorized their teachings. The disciples of Jesus must have committed themselves to intensive instruction. After they received special commissioning, they gave themselves to the Word of God and to preaching. The church followed the example of the disciples. It followed the teaching of Jesus by continuing steadfastly in the apostles' (disciples') teaching (see Acts 2:42; 6:2).

Before and after His resurrection Jesus indicated that His disciples would have authority to teach and build His church in His name (see Matthew 16:16-20; 28:18-20). As the Father had sent Jesus, Jesus sent the apostles (see John 20:21). In Jesus' name repentance and forgiveness were to be proclaimed (see Luke 24:47). All of these things were fulfilled in the early church because Jesus gave the Holy Spirit to the apostles. The Spirit brought events to their remembrance and led them into all truth (see John 14-17). In this way the Spirit of God led the apostles in ministry and mission. The apostles' words were confirmed by Jesus through the inspiration of the Spirit. Paul's commissioning to preaching and teaching was different from that of the other apostles, but Jesus' affirmation of Paul's work was quite similar (see Acts 9).[5] Therefore, there is good reason to believe that Jesus authenticated the work of the apostles in their work of writing Scripture. Following John W. Wenham, we seem justified in saying: "To Christ, his own teaching and the teaching of his Spirit-taught apostles were true, authoritative, inspired. To him, what he and they said under the direction of the Spirit,

God said. To him, the God of the New Testament was the living God; and in principle the teaching of the New Testament was the teaching of the living God."[6]

Jesus Christ: New Testament Scripture

We have seen that Jesus' authority was stamped on the New Testament writers. Now we will observe the New Testament's teaching about Jesus.

Over the past 200 years much debate in scholarly circles has wrestled with questions about Jesus. These discussions have led to the "quest for the historical Jesus," the "new quest for the historical Jesus," Christologies "from below," Christologies "from above," and now the so-called Jesus Seminar, which raises suspicion about the entire New Testament. This is not the place to evaluate the relationship between the Jesus of history and the picture presented of Him in the New Testament. But it seems clear to us that Jesus created the church; the church did not create Jesus. So the words of Jesus were not created by the church; the words of Jesus became the foundation for the church and its writings. We want to learn what the New Testament writers believed about Jesus. Our purpose in doing so is to help us establish a model for the written Word of God by looking at the living Word of God.

The apostle John proclaimed, "In the beginning was the Word, and the Word was with God, and the Word was God" (John 1:1). John identified the Word with Jesus (see John 1:14). Jesus has always been. He is eternal. He is God. Before His death He prayed, "Father, glorify me in your presence with that glory I had with you before the world existed" (John 17:5). His own prayer affirms His preexistence. These themes are echoed in the Epistles (see Philippians 2:5-8; Colossians 1:15-16). The claim to Jesus' preexistence is simultaneously a claim to His deity. When we point to Jesus, we say that He is God (see Hebrews 1:8; Romans 9:5). Not only does God live through Jesus and with Jesus, but also Jesus Himself is God (see John 1:1).

Yet Jesus is also portrayed as a man. His humanity is taken for granted in the Synoptic Gospels. Other points in the Bible seem to witness to His humanity in particular, as if it might have been called into question or its significance neglected.

Mark's Gospel focuses on Jesus' humanity. Luke and Matthew present the birth stories and some aspects of His human life. Luke even emphasizes Jesus' human development (see Luke 2:40, 52). John, more than any other writer, pictures Jesus' humanity. His humanity was like ours. It was visible for all to see (see John 1:14). As we have already noted, He was regarded as a rabbi (see John 1:38; 3:2; 9:2; 11:8). Jesus grew tired (see John 4:6), grew thirsty (see John 4:7), and displayed genuine emotions (see John 11:33-35). These are all traits of genuine humanity.

The New Testament identified Him as "Jesus of Nazareth" (Acts 2:22; 4:10; 22:8). He was seen, heard, and touched by His disciples (see 1 John 1:1-2). To deny Jesus' genuine humanity is viewed as heresy (see 1 John 4:2-3). Because of His humanity Jesus is able "to sympathize with our weaknesses." He "has been tempted in every way as we are, yet without sin" (Hebrews 4:15).

The early church confessed Jesus as a real man. Yet He was a unique man, as evidenced by His virgin birth and resurrection. His significance as a man is found not in comparison with or rank alongside other men but in contrast with others.[7]

In His complete humanity Jesus remained sinless. He always did the will of His Father (see John 10:37; 14:10; 15:10; 17:4). Jesus was called "the righteous one" (1 John 2:1), the "holy one" (Acts 2:27), "the light of the world" (John 8:12), and "Faithful and True" (Revelation 19:11). He knew no sin (see 2 Corinthians 5:21; 1 Peter 2:22). The New Testament simultaneously affirms His humanity, His real temptations (see Matthew 4:1-11), and His complete sinlessness. Unquestionably, the New Testament affirms His uniqueness. The total impression is that Jesus was recognized as fully God and fully man.

The tension created by this confession has created intense debate throughout church history. Some have emphasized one or the other. The result has been the introduction of unorthodox teachings. The deity of Christ has been denied by some (Ebionites, Arians). Others have denied the reality of His humanity, thinking that He only appeared to be man

(Docetists). Still others think that He was a man who was adopted as divine at His baptism. Combinations of these faulty views have claimed that Jesus is God, but His humanity is incomplete. Similarly, others have maintained His humanity but have been less than clear about His deity.

The classic Christian tradition has always claimed that Jesus Christ is fully God and perfect man. He is one person with two natures. The two natures are united in one person without forming a third nature or two separate persons.[8]

Conclusion

We have seen that the Old Testament looked forward to Jesus' coming. Jesus understood His life and ministry in light of the Old Testament. He lived in light of the truthfulness and authority of the Old Testament. Jesus Christ, the Son of God incarnate, who claimed divine authority for all He did and taught, not only affirmed the absolute authority of the Old Testament but also unreservedly submitted to it. His reading of the Old Testament was shaped by His own messianic mission. At the heart of Jesus' biblical interpretation was a Christocentric perspective. Jesus became the direct and primary source for the church's understanding of the Old Testament.

Jesus discipled and commissioned His followers to pass on His teaching. The Spirit of God was given to enable them for this task. The result was Spirit-directed writings that focused on the life, ministry, death, resurrection, and exaltation of Christ. The New Testament equally affirms the deity and humanity of Jesus. This picture of the living Word serves as a model for rightly viewing the written Word. This book will develop a Christological model for understanding Holy Scripture.

Our next chapters will present a view of the Bible as a divine-human Book. It evidences genuine human characteristics and divine superintending. As Jesus was fully human, He remained sinless, even though He genuinely struggled with temptation (see Hebrews 2:18; 4:15). Likewise, the Bible is a fully human Book yet completely truthful in all its affirmations.

Before moving to our next subject, a reminder will be helpful: Jesus

Christ is not merely a model for our view of the Bible or its interpretation. He is the main theme and goal of our study of Scripture. The focus is on Jesus. The Bible is important to illuminate His words and deeds rather than the reverse. Our study of the Bible begins from our belief in Christ and concludes with the building of our faith. Indeed, in all our theological pursuits, Jesus is the Alpha and Omega, the author and finisher of our faith.

Endnotes

[1]John W. Wenham, *Christ and the Bible* (Downers Grove: InterVarsity Press, 1972), 106-108.

[2]R.T. France, *Jesus and the Old Testament* (Downers Grove: InterVarsity Press, 1971), 75.

[3]John Rogerson, *The Study and Use of the Bible* (Grand Rapids: William B. Eerdmans Publishing Co., 1988), 5.

[4]C.K. Barrett, "The Old Testament in the New," *Cambridge History of the Bible*, 3 vols. (Cambridge: University Press, 1970), 1:405.

[5]See Wenham, *Christ and the Bible*, 109-23.

[6]Ibid., 123; also see L. Russ Bush, "On Taking the Bible Literally," *Authority and Interpretation: A Baptist Perspective*, ed. Duane A. Garrett and Richard R. Melick, Jr. (Grand Rapids: Baker Book House, 1987), 84-87.

[7]See Donald G. Bloesch, *Essentials of Evangelical Theology*, 2 vols. (San Francisco: Harper and Row, Publishers, Inc., 1978-79), 1:127-146.

[8]See H.D. McDonald, *Jesus—Human and Divine: An Introduction to Christology* (Grand Rapids: Zondervan Publishing House, 1968), and Carl F.H. Henry, ed., *Jesus of Nazareth: Saviour and Lord* (Grand Rapids: William B. Eerdmans, 1966).

CHAPTER 3

The Self-Witness of the Bible

Word Alert

Salvific—a term describing things pertaining to the salvation of men and women from the power and effects of sin.

Inspiration—the superintending influence the Holy Spirit exerted on the biblical writers, enabling them to communicate in the sacred writings the revelation of God.

Prophecy—the speaking, proclaiming, or announcing by prophets under the influence of divine inspiration. The primary ways the prophets received revelation included direct encounter with God, dreams, and visions. The sayings of prophets at times had direct application for their own settings, whereas at other times they are best understood as foretelling future events.

Apocalyptic—a type of prophetic literature that discloses the future. Its primary focus is overthrowing the present age and establishing God's rule.

What does the Bible claim for itself? To some critics, that question may seem unanswerable. One such critic has said:

> According to conservative arguments … the Bible … "claims" to be divinely inspired. All this is nonsense. There is no "the Bible" that claims to be divinely inspired, there is no "it" that

has a "view of itself." There is only this or that source, like 2 Timothy or 2 Peter, which makes statements about certain other writings, these rather undefined. There is no such thing as "the Bible's view of itself" from which a fully authoritative answer to these questions can be obtained.[1]

The critic's argument is certainly articulate but not devastating. In fact, more evidence than 2 Timothy 3:16 enriches our understanding of the nature of Scripture. Rather, a compounding of the biblical testimony, coupled with the inward work of the Holy Spirit, bears witness by and with the written Word of God in our hearts.[2] It is this confirming work of the Holy Spirit in the lives of believers that enables them to see the Bible as the written Word of God.

The approach of the Bible's self-witness or self-attestation is sometimes rejected on the grounds of circular reasoning. While the reasoning may seem circular, it is not a vicious circle. The circle is viable because it relates to God's salvific purpose (salvation). For the Scriptures, which affirm their own testimony, point us to Christ; and to see Christ, we must go to the Bible. Certainly, a place for additional testimony exists outside the Bible, but the Scripture's own claim must be given prior consideration. As with all points of theology, a consistent method would be to take seriously statements that Scripture makes about itself and then to formulate specific beliefs in light of those statements. That being the case, let us look at various ways Scripture speaks about itself.[3]

The Bible's Self-Witness: The Old Testament

Both Testaments view the words of Scripture as God's own words. Just as the Old Testament treats the Mosaic law as God's words (see 1 Kings 22:8-16; Nehemiah 8; Psalm 119), the Old Testament as a whole is seen as "the very words of God" (Romans 3:2), written by men whom the Holy Spirit moved and taught (see 1 Peter 1:10-12; 2 Peter 1:20-21). The Old Testament records several instances of speech from God to individuals. The most familiar example comes from the giving of the law on Mount Sinai. We read: "Then God spoke all these words: 'I am the Lord your God, who brought you out of the land of Egypt, out of the place of slavery. Do not have other gods besides me. … Do not covet … anything that belongs to your neighbor'" (Exodus 20:1-17; also see 20:22-23:33).

The Old Testament often pictures God as communicating with people by using actual spoken words, not just thoughts or ideas somehow communicated apart from words. The expected response to these words follows the Exodus pattern: "We will do everything that the Lord has commanded" (Exodus 24:3).

Numerous examples could be given of God's words to His people, God's words spoken by His people, or God's words written through His prophets. Psalm 119 exemplifies the reverence God's people held for God's Word. God's Word serves as a guide for godly living (see vv. 9-11), provides strength for the weary (see v. 28), gives instruction (see v. 33) and understanding (see v. 34), brings renewal to life (see v. 40), and leads to joy and delight (see vv. 35, 111). The psalmist described God's Word as more precious than silver and gold (see v. 72), right (see v. 128), wonderful (see v. 129), fully trustworthy (see v. 138), true (see v. 142), established (see v. 152), and eternal (see v. 160). The right response to God's Word is to love it and meditate on it all day long (see v. 97) because it is a lamp to our feet and a light for our path (see v. 105).

The Bible's Self Witness: The New Testament

This grand psalm, Psalm 119, which refers to the Word of God so often, reflects the great presupposition of all Christian preaching and teaching: reverence for what God has said in His Word. The way the New Testament speaks about the Old Testament makes this readily apparent. That which appears in the Old Testament is cited in the New Testament with formulas like "God says" and "the Holy Spirit says" (see Acts 4:24-25; 13:47; 2 Corinthians 6:16). Scripture and God are so closely joined together in the minds of the New Testament authors that they naturally could speak of Scripture doing what it records God doing (see Galatians 3:8). Likewise, Old Testament quotations or allusions are viewed not only as what Moses, David, Jeremiah, or Isaiah wrote but also as what they said through the Holy Spirit (see Mark 7:6; 12:36; Romans 11:9).

In keeping with New Testament practices, John's Gospel introduces statements or ideas from the Old Testament with the words "it is written" (John 6:31; 8:17; 12:14; 15:25). The Gospel employs this phrase to put "an end to all contradiction."[4] While some people view this as an overstatement, the authority resident in the appeal "it is written" is beyond dispute. Thus, the Gospel's expression "these are written" (John 20:31) intends to communicate that the same authority is present in John's message.

The New Testament clearly pictures the divine and authoritative character of the apostolic word (see Romans 1:5; 10:3; 16:26). The reference to the divine character of the apostolic word in its written and oral form calls for a response of faith and obedience like the Old Testament response previously described. When Paul taught and commanded in Christ's name (see 2 Thessalonians 3:6), he claimed Christ's authority because he was Christ's apostle (see 1 Corinthians 14:37). He maintained that both his words and ministry were Spirit-given (see 1 Corinthians 2:9-13). Thus, Paul offered a pattern of inspiration that called for the same perspective toward the apostolic writings, which became the New Testament, that the apostles had toward the Old Testament.

The Scripture, because of its divine content and origin, can be described as "trustworthy" (1 Timothy 1:15; 2 Timothy 2:11; Titus 3:8), "confirmed" (Hebrews 2:3), "eternal" (1 Peter 1:24-25), and "certain" (2 Peter 1:19). Those who build their lives on Scripture will not be disappointed (see Romans 9:33; 1 Peter 2:6). The Word was written to instruct and encourage (see Romans 15:4), to lead to saving faith (see 2 Timothy 3:15), to guide people toward godliness (see 2 Timothy 3:16), and to equip believers for good works (see 2 Timothy 3:17). God's people will know and hear God's Word (see 1 John 2:20, 27; 4:6), which "cannot be broken" (John 10:35).

Scripture's purpose is to lead men and women into a right relationship with God and to enable believers to glorify God in all of life's activities.

Scripture, however, is concerned not only with a person's spiritual needs but also with the nature, history, origin, and destination of humanity. Thus, the Bible teaches us to understand all of life under the providential control of God. The Bible is not only a Book of conversion but also a Book of creation and redemptive history. It is this perspective that best represents and defines the divine character of Scripture.

Central to Scripture is the unifying history of God's redeeming words and acts, of which the life and work of Jesus Christ serve as the ultimate focus. Yet God acts at three related levels. The first is the public stage of history, which included a series of redemptive events, predictions, and explanations at various stages along the way. These acts and words emerged at a second level with written public records, which we have in Holy Scripture. These records included narratives, celebrations, apocalyptic material, letters, wisdom sayings, and historical explanations, all of which communicated God's ongoing work of grace. The third level is the human response and understanding of God's work as the Holy Spirit illuminates human hearts and minds to interpret the sacred writings.

Jesus Christ binds and unites everything in Scripture—beginning and end, creation and redemption, humanity, the fall, history, and the future. If this overriding unity is neglected, Scripture can become denatured, losing its "theological-Christological definition" and becoming abstracted from the peculiar nature and content of Scripture.[5] Numerous other passages could be cited that indicate the Bible's self-witness to its divine character (see Psalm 19:7-11; Luke 24:25-27; Hebrews 1:1-2; 2 Peter 3:16). Our representative survey, however, shows that the Bible's witness to its own inspiration and authority is found throughout the Scriptures. Second Timothy 3:16-17, "All Scripture is inspired by God and is profitable for teaching, for rebuking, for correcting, for training in righteousness, so that the man of God may be complete, equipped for every good work," is a very specific claim of biblical inspiration and authority. We will examine this important passage and its witness to the Bible's inspiration in a later chapter. Now we will examine the prophetic formula "thus says the Lord."

The Bible's Self-Witness: Thus Says The Lord

An exhaustive survey of the prophetic formula "thus says the Lord" or "the word of the Lord came to me saying" would be impossible. We are thus limited to some typical examples. When we turn to the Book of Jeremiah, we find this opening statement:

> The word of the Lord came to me: "I chose you before I formed you in the womb; I set you apart before you were born. I appointed you a prophet to the nations." But I protested, "Oh no, Lord God! Look, I don't know how to speak since I am only a youth." Then the Lord said to me: "Do not say, 'I am only a youth,' for you will go to everyone I send you to and speak whatever I tell you. Do not be afraid of anyone, for I will be with you to rescue you. This is the Lord's declaration." Then the Lord reached out his hand, touched my mouth, and told me: "I have now filled your mouth with my words" (Jeremiah 1:4-9).

The book continues with accounts and examples of how the words of God came to Jeremiah, including what God said. Also, we find accounts of things God told Jeremiah to do and how he did them, together with accounts of what Jeremiah said to God and stories about Jeremiah, sometimes in the third person.

The frequent use of this introductory formula in the writings of Jeremiah and the other prophets indicates the high degree of authority and reliability claimed for the words the prophets spoke in God's name.[6] Scholars have shown that such a formula would have been used in the Ancient Near East to introduce an edict issued by a king to his subjects.

We can see the resident authority inherent in these words. When the Bible uses the words "thus says the Lord" hundreds of times, the phrase is understood as a royal message from a sovereign king to His subjects. The message could not be challenged; it could only be obeyed. God is presented as the sovereign King of Israel. When the prophets speak, they are bringing the divine King's completely authoritative decrees to His subjects.

The royal-decree formula is employed in the Old Testament's description of the conflict between Sennacherib, the king of Assyria, and Yahweh, the King of Israel, in Isaiah 36-37. Other examples of this formula can be found in the report of Pharaoh's edict (see Exodus 4-5) and in the message of Ben-Hadad (see 1 Kings 20). Disastrous results came to a false prophet who adopted the formula in Jeremiah 28:2, 11, 17.

Thus, the Bible insists that God not only addresses humankind universally through nature, history, and the reason and conscience of men and women but also addresses His word to and through certain persons in special ways. Over and over again, God is identified as a speaking God who reveals His message to a specific individual in a unique place at a particular time. In addition to the introduction in Jeremiah's prophecy, another example is, "The word of the Lord that came to Hosea son of Beeri during the reigns of Uzziah, Jotham, Ahaz, and Hezekiah, kings of Judah, and of Jeroboam son of Jehoash, king of Israel" (Hosea 1:1). A similar example is found in Micah 1:1: "The word of the Lord that came to Micah the Moreshite—what he saw regarding Samaria and Jerusalem in the days of Jotham, Ahaz, and Hezekiah, kings of Judah."

Likewise, in Joel 1:1 and Zephaniah 1:1 the expression serves as a covering phrase or a title for collections of written communication. The written words are as authoritative and potent as the prophet's spoken words. For instance, the prophet Jeremiah does full justice to the dynamic vitality of God's Word (*dabar*) yet declares that Yahweh's words are to be recorded on a scroll (Jeremiah 36:2-3). The prophet writes with the hope that the people of God will turn from their wicked ways. The written word, therefore, may be viewed as no less potent than the spoken word. Indeed, Jeremiah betrays no reluctance to identify as the divine word what the prophet himself asserts. Whether God or Jeremiah is identified as the spokesman, the written account is characterized as the word of the Lord. The prophets have an absolute conviction that the origin and authority of their message come from God (see Numbers 12:8; 23:5; Jeremiah 1:9).[7]

The Pentateuch includes the written law, the words of the covenant, and much else that is related to the word of the Lord. The concept of the Word of God as written revelation was in force from Mosaic times. There is no hint that a written form undercut the dynamic force of the word of God (see Exodus 31:18; Deuteronomy 4:13; 5:22; 9:10). The written documents, maintaining the character of decisive testimony and witness, occupy a prominent place with respect to God's covenant with Israel (see Deuteronomy 31:22).

As we noted in the previous chapter, Jesus honored the Old Testament. His attitude prepared the way for the apostles' respect for Scripture. The apostles, although aware that the Old Testament prophets did not always know the full meaning of their oracles (see 1 Peter 1:10-12), understood that what was written in the past was useful to teach their generation and those to follow (see Romans 15:4; 1 Corinthians 10:11; 2 Timothy 3:16). The written Word carries the same dynamic force and authority as the spoken word. This conclusion is confirmed by the fulfillment of prophecy.

The Bible's Self-Witness: Fulfilled Prophecy

Jesus' references to the necessity of fulfilled prophecy are numerous. It is not always easy to discern the principles of interpretation that govern our Lord's reading of prophecy. Before looking at our Lord's words and deeds, perhaps a brief word about the main types of Old Testament prophecy will prove helpful. The primary writing prophets (4 major and 12 minor) are well known. In addition, as we have seen, others carried out this significant role. Moses, who wrote the law of God, was regarded as a prophet without equal (see Deuteronomy 34:10-12). Prophetic voices were also present during the period of the judges (see Judges 2:1-5; 3:9-11; 4:4; 6:8). Samuel came as a second Moses (see Jeremiah 15:1; Psalm 99:6), and His work continued through Gad and Nathan (see 2 Samuel 12:25; 24:11). After the separation of the 10 tribes, Ahijah (see 1 Kings 11:29), Elijah (see 1 Kings 18-19), and Elisha (see 2 Kings 5) carried on the prophetic line.

These prophecies concerned the internal destiny of Israel, the promise of Messiah, and predictions about the last days. Sometimes these elements were blended together. At other times their meaning was clear only after the unfolding of history.[8]

Examples of prophecies related to the internal destiny of Israel include the announcement of the northern kingdom's exile by Hosea, Amos, and Micah. Similarly, Isaiah, Jeremiah, and Ezekiel foretold events about the exile of the southern kingdom in Babylon.

Numerous prophecies focused on the advent of Christ. The matters of interpreting these prophecies "serve only to throw into stronger relief the implied God-givenness of the whole body of prophetic writings which by divine necessity must be fulfilled."[9] The fact that the relationship between some prophecies and their fulfillment is not immediately obvious to the readers of the prophecies only makes their fulfillment more remarkable. One fact is sure: Jesus' life was guided by a sense of divine destiny marked out by the fulfillment of the Scriptures.

Among dozens of passages that could be selected, some of the more important references to His teaching about the fulfillment of prophecy include:

"Today as you listen, this Scripture has been fulfilled" (Luke 4:21).

"This is the one about whom it is written: 'See, I am sending my messenger ahead of you; he will prepare your way before you'" (Luke 7:27).

"Elijah does come first and restores all things ... just as it is written about him" (Mark 9:12-13).

Then he took the Twelve aside and told them, "See, we are going up to Jerusalem. Everything that is written through the prophets about the Son of Man will be accomplished. For he will be handed over to the Gentiles, and he will be mocked, insulted, spit on; and after they flog him, they will kill him, and he will rise on the third day" (Luke 18:31-33).

"These are days of vengeance to fulfill all the things that are written" (Luke 21:22).

He replied, "The one who dipped his hand with me in the bowl—he will betray me. The Son of Man will go just as it is written about him…" (Matthew 26:23-24).

"For I tell you, what is written must be fulfilled in me: 'And he was counted among the lawless.' Yes, what is written about me is coming to its fulfillment" (Luke 22:37).

Then Jesus said to them, "Tonight all of you will fall away because of me, for it is written: 'I will strike the shepherd, and the sheep of the flock will be scattered'" (Matthew 26:31).

"Or do you think that I cannot call on my Father, and he will provide me here and now with more than twelve legions of angels? How, then, would the Scriptures be fulfilled that say it must happen this way?" At that time Jesus said to the crowds, "Have you come out with swords and clubs, as if I were a criminal, to capture me? Every day I used to sit, teaching in the temple, and you didn't arrest me. But all this has happened so that the writings of the prophets would be fulfilled" (Matthew 26:53-56).

"How foolish you are, and how slow to believe all that the prophets have spoken! Wasn't it necessary for the Messiah to suffer these things and enter into his glory?" Then beginning with Moses and all the Prophets, he interpreted for them the things concerning himself in all the Scriptures (Luke 24:25-27).

"These are my words that I spoke to you while I was still with you—that everything written about me in the Law of Moses, the Prophets, and the Psalms must be fulfilled." Then he opened their minds to understand the Scriptures. He also said to them, "This is what is written: 'The Messiah would suffer and rise from the dead the third day, and repentance for forgiveness of sins would be proclaimed in his name to all the nations, beginning at Jerusalem'" (Luke 24:44-47).

"You pore over the Scriptures because you think you have eternal life in them, and yet they testify about me. But you are not willing to come to me so that you may have life. ... Do not think that I will accuse you to the Father. Your accuser is Moses, on whom you have set your hope. For if you believed Moses, you would believe me, because he wrote about me. But if you don't believe what he wrote, how will you believe my words?" (John 5:39-47).

"I'm not speaking about all of you; I know those I have chosen. But the Scripture must be fulfilled: 'The one who eats my bread has raised his heel against me'" (John 13:18).

"If I had not done the works among them that no one else has done, they would not be guilty of sin. Now they have seen and hated both me and my Father. But this happened so that the statement written in their law might be fulfilled: 'They hated me for no reason'" (John 15:24-25).

"While I was with them, I was protecting them by your name that you have given me. I guarded them and not one of them is lost, except the son of destruction, so that the Scripture may be fulfilled" (John 17:12).

Jesus' understanding of the events in His life as the fulfillment of the prophetic word can be clearly observed. His acceptance of the authoritative character of prophetic Scripture is likewise clear and complete.[10]

Conclusion

The Scripture's own testimony of its divine nature and authoritative character is revealed through a variety of means. We recognize these truths through the witness of the Old Testament; the witness of the New Testament; the prophetic shape of portions of Scripture; and the fulfillment of prophecy in Israel, in the church, and ultimately in the life of our Lord. The attitude of Jesus toward Scripture provides a working model for our lives as we seek to live conscious of God's leadership and obedient to the teaching of Scripture.

Prophecies and Fulfillment		
Old Testament Passages	New Testament Passages	Subject
Psalm 110:1	Matthew 22:43-44	The Davidic reign and exaltation of Jesus Christ
Malachi 4:5-6	Matthew 11:14; 17:12	John the Baptist as the prophesied Elijah
Isaiah 61:1-2	Luke 4:18-21	Jesus Christ's mission of mercy and justice
Isaiah 6:9-10	Luke 8:10	The refusal of many to follow/obey Christ
Psalm 118:22-23	Matthew 21:42; Acts 4:11; 1 Peter 2:7-8	The rejection of Christ
Isaiah 53	Mark 9:12; Luke 24:25, 46	Jesus Christ's sufferings

Zechariah 13:7	Mark 14:27, 48-49	The disciples' lack of courage and the arrest of Jesus
Psalm 41:9	John 13:18	The betrayal of Jesus
Psalm 16:8-11	Acts 2:25-28	Jesus Christ's resurrection
Isaiah 49:6	Luke 24:47	The universal proclamation of the Gospel

Endnotes

[1] James Barr, *Fundamentalism* (London: S.C.M. Press Ltd., 1977), 78.

[2] See John Calvin, *Institutes of the Christian Religion*, ed. John T. McNeill, 2 vols. (Philadelphia: The Westminster Press, 1960), 1:75-80.

[3] Much of the information in this chapter can be found in David S. Dockery, "The Divine-Human Authorship of Inspired Scripture," *Authority and Interpretation: A Baptist Perspective*, ed. Duane A. Garrett and Richard R. Melick, Jr. (Grand Rapids: Baker Book House, 1987), 13-43. Also see the lengthy discussion by Wayne A. Grudem, "Scripture's Self-Attestation and the Problem of Formulating a Doctrine of Scripture," *Scripture and Truth*, ed. D.A. Carson and John D. Woodbridge (Grand Rapids: Zondervan Publishing House, 1983), 19-59.

[4] Herman Ridderbos, *Studies in Scripture and Its Authority* (Grand Rapids: William B. Eerdmans Publishing Company, 1978), 21.

[5] Ibid., 25.

[6] See Walther Eichrodt, *Theology of the Old Testament*, trans. J.A. Baker, 2 vols. (London: S.C.M. Press, Ltd., 1961-67), 1:340.

[7] See the discussion in Dewey M. Beegle, *Scripture, Tradition, and Infallibility* (Grand Rapids: William B. Eerdmans Publishing Co., 1973), 25-28, and Carl F.H. Henry, "The Authority and Inspiration of the Bible," *The Expositor's Bible Commentary*, ed. Frank E. Gaebelein, 12 vols. (Grand Rapids: Zondervan Publishing House, 1979), 1:13-22.

[8]See William Dyrness, *Themes in Old Testament Theology* (Downers Grove: InterVarsity Press, 1979), 211-24.

[9]John W. Wenham, *Christ and the Bible* (Downers Grove: InterVarsity Press, 1972), 25.

[10]Ibid., 25-26.

CHAPTER 4

The Divine-Human Authorship of the Bible

Word Alert

Canonical—a term referring to the 66 books of the Old Testament and the New Testament that have been recognized and accepted by the church as authoritative and inspired by God. Meaning *rule* or *measuring rod*, the term *canon* refers to the church's rule for faith and practice.

Docetic view of Scripture—a view suggesting that the human authorship of Scripture is only apparent or imaginative.

Progressive revelation—a term indicating that God's self-disclosure unfolds and develops over time. This revelation interprets and amplifies the previous revelation but does not contradict it in any way.

Textual criticism—a discipline that attempts to reconstruct the original text of the Scriptures as closely as can be determined.

We have learned that the Bible witnesses to its own divine character. Yet our earlier observations revealed that over 40 human authors wrote in a variety of ways, using diverse languages in different societies and in different geographical locations over a period of more than 1,000 years. In this chapter we will learn how these human authors in their own contexts and with their own styles, abilities, and personalities penned the Word of God. We will also discuss how a divine word can be communicated in human language.

The Bible's Authorship: Prevailing Beliefs

Every Lord's Day Christians around the world in churches of various denominations gather to hear the Bible read and expounded. What is true in these congregations is characteristic of many Baptist churches, as well. It is common in these churches to hear such phrases as "Let us stand together as we read the Word of God." As indicated in chapter 1, that which is assumed by many faithful believers—that the Bible is a divine Word—has become a major problem for many who struggle with what it means to say that the Bible is the written Word of God.

A large number of present-day Christians have been taught in their homes and churches to believe that the Bible is a divinely inspired Book, written by godly men. They believe that the Bible is God's revelation to men and women; and since it is God's revelation, it is to be studied and obeyed. A characteristic response among these faithful believers is, "The Bible says it; I believe it; that settles it." Such people gladly accept the biblical reports that Jonah was swallowed by a fish, that an ax head floated on the water, that Jesus walked on water, and that He was raised from the dead on the third day.

Conversely, others who have been influenced by trends in contemporary philosophy and theology have great difficulty accepting these biblical accounts as miraculous without reinterpreting them. Although many have difficulty believing the miraculous accounts, they nevertheless confess the Bible as an important Book. For these people the Bible is essentially a human Book. It is important because it is a record of humanity's quest of and experience with God. Most Christians, including most Baptists, would want to confess more than this limited affirmation, maintaining that God in some way reveals Himself through the collection of human books. Even though the books may seem to some to be contradictory, the readers believe that they can still hear God's truth through the writings.

Between these positions are numerous opinions that try to explain carefully and fairly the two-sided character of the Bible as a divine-human Book. These views attempt to do justice to the mystery of Scripture's divine inspiration and still maintain its human authorship. One of the key issues in developing a doctrine of Scripture is the need to maintain with equal force both the divinity and humanity of the Bible. The precise relationship between divine revelation and the human writings that comprise the canonical Scripture has been and will continue to be a subject of contention.[1]

The Bible's Authorship: Divine and Human

Scripture cannot be understood correctly unless we take into consideration that it has a dual-sided authorship. It is not enough to affirm that the Bible is a human witness to divine revelation, because the Bible is also God's witness to Himself. An affirmation that Scripture is partly the Word of God and partly the words of humans is inadequate. What must be affirmed is that the Bible is entirely and completely the Word of God as well as the words of the human authors (see Acts 4:25).[2]

A Balanced View of the Bible's Authorship

It is not entirely appropriate to make a direct correspondence between Scripture and Jesus Christ; but nevertheless, there is an observable analogy. The doctrine of the incarnation does account for the true activity of God in the human dimension, thus allowing for at least the possibility that God could work in human beings to communicate His Word in human words. The Holy Spirit is the one who, in a mystery for which the incarnation provides the only analogy, causes the verbal human witness to coincide with God's witness to Himself.[3] Just as the conception of Jesus came by the miraculous overshadowing of the Holy Spirit (see Luke 1:35), Scripture is the product of the Spirit's inspiration (see 2 Timothy 3:16). Likewise, as Jesus took on human form through a human mother, the Bible has come to us in human language through human authors. The result is that Jesus is the living Word of God, the God-man; and the Bible is the written Word of God, the divine-human Scripture.

An affirmation that Scripture is completely the Word of God and the very words of humans also points to its dual-sided nature. Because it is the Word of the infinite, all-knowing, eternal God, it speaks eternal truth that is applicable to readers of all time beyond the original recipients. Yet at the same time, it is the word from godly men to specific communities, addressing problems and situations within certain contexts and cultures.

Some claim that the Bible is primarily, if not entirely, a human product of an illumined religious consciousness.[4] Such a view maintains the possibility that the Bible could lead its readers to divine truth but denies that the Bible is a revelation of divine truth. By comparison with the heretical views in the early statements about Christ, we could classify this position as Ebionitic, a view that stresses the humanity of Christ while losing sight of His essential deity.[5] On the other hand, many have emphasized the divine aspect of Scripture so predominantly that the human element is only an outward appearance of the divine. Such an approach denies the Bible's genuine humanity, as well as its historicity. Again, parallel to the unorthodox views of the person of Christ, the latter view has tendencies toward a Docetic view of Scripture.[6]

We can see the importance of affirming a balanced view of Scripture. But how does the Christian community maintain such a balance? How can it be affirmed that Scripture is the inspired Word of God when it is a collection of books by human authors? How is it possible that the Bible can simultaneously be the Word of God and a human composition? It is to these questions that the remainder of this chapter is addressed.

The Human Authorship of Holy Scripture

Both the activity of the Spirit and the activities and circumstances of the human writers must be taken seriously. The biblical writers employed the linguistic resources available to them as they wrote to specific people with particular needs at particular times. The human authors were not lifted from their culture or removed from their contexts. They were not autonomous but were active participants among God's covenant people. They were aware of God's presence and leadership in their lives. Whether or not they were all fully aware that they were writing inspired Scripture, they certainly demonstrated a God-consciousness.[7] Obviously, the writers were not unbiased historical observers; they were men strongly committed to faith. Thus, the concursive action (a flowing together) of the Holy Spirit and human authorship is reinforced by the spiritual commitments of the writers.

Human authors and cultural-temporal distance. It is certainly true that the biblical writers were limited to their own contexts; yet they share similarities that transcend times and places. The primary similarity is one the writers share with all human beings, since all men and women have been created in God's image (see Genesis 1:26-27) and, as a result, share certain common characteristics. As theologians since the time of Augustine have observed, human beings created in the image of God can have memories of the past, considerations of the present, and expectations for the future. To the extent that these potential capacities are employed, persons—unlike objects—are not bound by culture or time. The writers are certainly time-related but not necessarily time-bound. Moses and Paul, among others, demonstrated cross-cultural influences and experiences. The writers were certainly not entirely culturally or behaviorally conditioned. Even though they were obviously influenced by the time and culture in which they wrote, the writers freely rejected some concepts of their culture and freely endorsed others.[8]

Eugene A. Nida has observed that humans created in God's image can develop the ability to think and communicate in linguistic symbols. Therefore, communication is possible among the diverse linguistic cultures of the world for three reasons:

1. The processes of human reasoning are essentially the same, irrespective of cultural diversity.
2. All peoples have a common range of experience.
3. All peoples possess the capacity for at least some adjustment to the way others use symbols and words.[9]

We do not wish to press these assertions beyond their limits.

Nevertheless, a revelation written through a human author in a particular language, whether Greek, Hebrew, or Aramaic, can be intelligible to those who know other languages. God can communicate with humans who have been created in His image. Likewise, humans can communicate with other humans across cultures and time. By maintaining these observations about humanity, we can affirm the genuine humanness of Scripture without denying that God can speak through divine-human Scripture.

Some have concluded that time and cultural differences make the Bible basically unusable today. Yet we believe, on the basis of the commonalities outlined above, that God's revelation can be communicated through human authors who lived 2,000 years ago in various cultures. "We must resist a misuse of the principle of cultural relatedness as a cloak to evade what the Scriptures really want to teach," claims Clark H. Pinnock.[10] Likewise, it is true that God's Word comes to us in human language and that it has features incidental to its teaching purposes. "But in 'all things necessary' that the Bible wishes to teach us it is true and coherent and possesses the wisdom of God."[11]

The biblical text is indeed the words of human authors in temporal-cultural contexts, but this does not limit the plausibility that God's eternal revelation can be communicated through their writings to contemporary men and women. We fully recognize the humanness and historicity of the biblical text. Simultaneously, we acknowledge that God's revelation can be, and indeed has been, communicated through this situation. The fact that the biblical authors were men of faith addresses the issue of concursive inspiration—that is, the way the Spirit used the activities and circumstances of human authors to write Holy Scripture. Moreover, recognition that every person bears the image of God helps us understand how communication can take place across cultures and ages.

Variety in the human message. Sometimes an overemphasis on the human authorship tends to focus primarily on the variety and diversity of beliefs and theologies among the biblical writers. A belief in the unity of the biblical message, affirmed in the previous chapters, is often lacking in those who overemphasize the human aspect of Scripture. Yet the concept of the overall unity, characteristic of historic Baptist and evangelical theology, emerges from a balanced view of inspiration. The balanced divine-human authorship of Scripture, coupled with the overriding themes of redemptive history, forms the basis for recognizing the theological unity in the Bible. We need to affirm not only the Bible's unity but also its very real variety. The different authors wrote from various contexts and situations. Each brought a particular theological emphasis to his writings.

The writers employed various types of literature to shape their messages. Likewise, the form in which the teaching is expressed is influenced by the literary type. The types of literature, whether legal, historic, poetic, prophetic, Gospel, epistolary, or apocalyptic, have distinctive characteristics. From the varied collection of writings came the basic prophetic-apostolic message.

We find not only a variety of types of literature but often variety within a particular type. In the Gospels we find parables, prophecies, narratives, history, and miracle stories, among others. Also, the different theological emphases among the Synoptic Gospel writers indicate the variety even within the Gospels themselves. Matthew's Kingdom theology differs from Mark's servant theology, and each is different from Luke's stress on Jesus as Savior of the world. Yet the central unity of Jesus Christ and the developing history of redemption cannot be ignored.[12]

Beyond this matter is the very real possibility of theological development within the Old and New Testaments and even within the individual authors.[13] Donald Guthrie's succinct comments on this difficult issue are extremely appropriate:

> The idea of progressive revelation is familiar in OT interpretation and also in the area of the relation of the OT.... With Christ the OT ritual system became obsolete, as the epistle to the Hebrews makes clear.... One obvious area where this [development in the New Testament] is undeniable is the

difference between the gospels and the rest of the NT. Before the death and resurrection of Christ the revelation given to the disciples was limited. In the nature of the case Jesus could not give a full explanation of his own death to his disciples until they had grasped the fact of it. But after the resurrection the apostolic preachers were guided into an understanding of it, although again not in any stereotyped way, but with a rich variety.[14]

The differences among the writers themselves and the development (seen as progressive revelation from the divine perspective) occurring in the Testaments and even in some of the writers themselves, such as Isaiah or Paul, point to the genuine humanness of the biblical text. Diversity, or variety in the sense of variations, is found in the expression of the central message of the Gospel. Yet the basis of unity is located in the oneness of the Gospel message. Therefore, variety works within the limits of the Gospel.

We must recognize that variety does not imply contradiction. The different writers, with their own emphases, varied their expressions according to their unique purposes and settings. But within this genuine and very rich variety, reflecting the true humanness of Scripture, is an authentic unity that results from the divine, superintending work of the Holy Spirit's inspiration.

The Bible's Authorship: Improper Deductions

Sometimes people reach improper conclusions from the data that has been presented in this chapter. Five common, yet improper, conclusions are reached about the human authorship of Scripture. Let us briefly examine these issues.

The Phenomena of Scripture

The Bible generally represents things as they appear (phenomena). For example, the Bible refers to a sunrise when, in fact, we all know that the earth rotates on its axis; the sun does not rise. Yet the weather report tells us what time we can expect tomorrow's sunrise. Why do we speak this way? Because we are describing things as they appear. It is no mistake or error in Scripture when the biblical writers do the same. The Bible is a Book of events and communication from common, everyday people. It is not a technical treatise of weather or other areas of science. The great Baptist theologian A.H. Strong asked, "Would it be preferable, in the O.T., if we should read: 'When the revolution of the earth upon its axis caused the rays of the solar luminary to impinge horizontally upon the retina, Isaac went out to meditate' (Genesis 24:63)?"[15]

It is illogical to assume that the Bible contains errors because the human authors reported things in a way contrary to reality. If the Bible taught that things appear one way, but they did not appear that way, we would probably agree that it could be an error. If the Bible taught that things are one way, but they were not that way, that too could be considered an error. But for the Bible to teach that things appear one way, when they actually are another way, is hardly an error. It reflects the genuine humanness of Scripture.

The Accommodation of Scripture

John Calvin used expressions like "God must speak baby talk for humans to understand His Word." He meant that God accommodated Himself to the level and culture of the Bible's original recipients. It is true that the Bible represents God as accommodating Himself to human language. But this recognition does not occasion the conclusion that accommodation to human language must involve accommodation to human error and that therefore the Bible contains error. An example concerns the biblical phrase "God repents." Some say that this must be an error, since God is unchangeable. The Bible does not present God as changing His actions to be consistent with His overall will or purpose, because His will or purpose does not change. The Bible pictures God as repenting because that is how it appears to the human authors. This does not suggest contradiction or error in Scripture when it is rightly understood as accommodation to human language.

The Salvation Emphasis

As we have seen in earlier chapters, special revelation is primarily redemptive. Second Timothy 3:15 says that the Holy Scriptures make us wise for salvation. Obviously, the salvation message is the focal point of Scripture. But it does not follow that because the Bible stresses one thing, it errs in lesser emphases. For example, it is not proper to conclude that because the Bible emphasizes salvation, it can be trusted on that matter, but that since it does not stress history, it may err in historical details.

Textual Criticism

Textual criticism is the science of determining the truest biblical reading by comparing one historical text with other historical texts. Often textual critics decide that a certain verse or group of verses is an untrue reading; that is, they doubt that it was a part of the oldest manuscripts. Examples of these kinds of passages include John 7:53-8:11; Mark 16:9-20; and the doxology or conclusion to the Lord's Prayer. Because scholars examine a text and decide that it does not belong to the Bible, some conclude that the Bible errs. Questioning the ending of Mark's Gospel does not imply that this Gospel is in error. Textual criticism points us to the truthfulness of the genuine or authentic text.

Sinful Humanity

We have seen that the Bible was written by men. Even though these men were faithful believers, they were not sinless. Yet it does not follow that since God inspired these humans to write Scripture, He would be incapable of keeping them free of human error in their writing. We know that King David was an adulterer, but we cannot infer that the Psalms therefore contain error. God's Spirit could certainly keep those Psalms free of human error.

These common misconceptions or objections are really improper conclusions that develop from an imbalanced view of Scripture. We cannot in any way ignore the human authorship of Scripture. But neither can we stress only the humanness of Scripture and ignore its divine inspiration. A proper understanding of the Bible demands a balanced view of the divine-human authorship.

Conclusion

The Bible as a divine-human Book is indeed special. But that means that it must be treated as equal to and yet more than an ordinary book. We must study the Bible through the use of literary and critical methodologies. To deny that kind of study would treat the Bible as less than human, less than historical, and less than literature. The Bible is a literary work that is both human and historical yet simultaneously the very Word of God. We will now turn our attention to the inspiration and dependability of Scripture, including various explanations of the divine-human authorship of Scripture.

Endnotes

[1] Most of the information in this chapter is found in David S. Dockery, "The Divine-Human Authorship of Inspired Scripture," *Authority and Interpretation: A Baptist Perspective*, ed. Duane A. Garrett and Richard R. Melick, Jr. (Grand Rapids: Baker Book House, 1987), 13-43.

[2] See Donald G. Bloesch, *Essentials of Evangelical Theology*, 2 vols. (San Francisco: Harper and Row, Publishers, Inc., 1978-79), 1:51-56.

[3] See David S. Dockery, "The Inerrancy and Authority of Scripture: Affirmations and Clarifications," *Theological Educator*, 37 (1988), 24, and John M. Frame, "The Spirit and the Scriptures," *Hermeneutics, Authority, and Canon*, ed. D.A. Carson and John D. Woodbridge (Grand Rapids: Zondervan Publishing House, 1986), 213-35.

[4] Gene M. Tucker and Douglas A. Knight, eds., *Humanizing America's Iconic Book* (Chico, California: Scholars Press, 1980).

[5] Bloesch, *Evangelical Theology*, 1:134.

[6] Ibid., 134-35, and John Gerstner, "The Church's Doctrine of Biblical Inspiration," *The Foundation of Biblical Authority*, ed. James M. Boice (Grand Rapids: Zondervan Publishing House, 1978), 12.

[7]See Millard J. Erickson, *Christian Theology*, 3 vols. (Grand Rapids: Baker Book House, 1983-86), 1:204-6.

[8]Gordon R. Lewis, "The Human Authorship of Inspired Scripture," *Inerrancy*, ed. Norman L. Geisler (Grand Rapids: Zondervan Publishing House, 1980), 240-46.

[9]Eugene A. Nida, *Message and Mission* (New York: Harper and Row, Publishers, Inc., 1960), 90.

[10]Clark H. Pinnock, *The Scripture Principle* (San Francisco: Harper and Row, Publishers, Inc., 1984), 110.

[11]Ibid., 115.

[12]See George E. Ladd, *A Theology of the New Testament* (Grand Rapids: William B. Eerdmans Publishing Co., 1974), 13-210, and Leon Morris, *New Testament Theology* (Grand Rapids: Zondervan Publishing House, 1986), 91-221. These different emphases point to the possible and helpful use of redaction criticism as a tool for theological interpretation of the Gospels.

[13]See Richard N. Longenecker, "On the Concept of Development in Pauline Thought," *Perspectives in Evangelical Theology*, ed. K. Kantzer and S.N. Gundry (Grand Rapids: Baker Book House, 1979), 195-200.

[14]Donald Guthrie, *New Testament Theology* (Downers Grove: InterVarsity Press, 1981), 51.

[15]Augustus Hopkins Strong, *Systematic Theology* (Old Tappan, New Jersey, 1907), 223.

CHAPTER 5

The Inspiration of the Bible

Word Alert

Theopneustos—a Greek term translated *divinely inspired* or *God-breathed* (2 Timothy 3:16), indicating that the Scriptures are the product of God's creative breath and thus divine.

Concursive inspiration—a term communicating that inspired Scriptures are at the same time divine and human words. Since Scripture has a dual authorship, it is the product of God as well as of human authors.

Contextual—a term denoting that some portions of Scripture have adapted certain life situations or cultural or temporal contexts to communicate their message.

Linguistics—the scientific study of language.

Enlightenment philosophy—a philosophical movement during the 17th and 18th centuries, sometimes identified as the Age of Reason. Characterized by rationalism and self-sufficiency, it rejected external authorities as the Bible, the church, and the state.

Plenary—a Latin term meaning *full*. When applied to the concept of inspiration, it means that the Bible is inspired in *all* its parts.

The term *divine inspiration* does not necessarily mean that the men who spoke and wrote inspired Scripture were temporarily stripped of their limitations in knowledge, memory, language, and ability to express themselves in specific contexts during certain periods of history. What, then, does *inspiration* mean? How does inspiration relate to the matter of divine-human authorship? How does inspiration relate to revelation? This chapter will attempt to deal with these questions by describing and defining the theological concept of inspiration. In doing do, it will also examine the various historical viewpoints on inspiration.

The Inspired Word: Inspiration and Revelation

In chapter 1 we learned that when God reveals Himself, He does so at least in part by revealing information about Himself. It is only by revelation that we know God. But the concept of revelation is only part of the answer to the problem of the knowledge of God. If all persons are to have an opportunity to know God, there must be a way to make this special revelation available to all persons. If this were not the case, revelation could be lost and become ineffective. There are two possible responses to this potential problem. One possibility would be for the revelation to be repeated time and time again to each generation. The other possibility would be somehow to preserve the revelation that has been given. God has employed the second method, which we call inspiration.

By *inspiration* we mean that through the superintending influence of God's Spirit on the writers of Holy Scripture, the account and interpretation of God's revelation have been recorded as God intended so that the Bible is actually the Word of God. Inspiration preserved or recorded what God had revealed so that the resulting document carried the same authority and effect as if God Himself were speaking directly. This view of complete inspiration, involving the divine intention and the words of Scripture, is called plenary inspiration.

The need for this record is apparent. Certainly, God could have chosen the process of oral retelling to preserve His revelation. Indeed, an aspect of the inspiration process included the use of oral sources. A dependable and reliable source of truth requires preservation in written form. So God's self-manifestation has been preserved through the Holy Spirit's work of inspiration.[1] Let us now turn our attention to the biblical teaching about inspiration.

The Inspired Word: Biblical Claims

Several important passages, in addition to those identified in chapter 3, help us understand the Bible's view of its own inspiration (see Psalm 19; 119; Luke 24:25-27; John 10:34-35; Hebrews 1:1-3; 2 Peter 3:16). The primary witness of the Bible to its own inspiration, however, is found in 2 Timothy 3:16-17: "All Scripture is inspired by God and is profitable for teaching, for rebuking, for correcting, for training in righteousness, so that the man of God may be complete, equipped for every good work."

The term *inspiration* (*theopneustos*) has a long heritage, but it is always used with additional explanation. This is because *theopneustos* is best translated as *God-breathed*. In contemporary usage the term *inspiration* suggests the idea of breathing into. The secular understanding of *inspiration* is generally synonymous with *illumination* or *human genius*. But the New Testament emphasis is that God breathed out what the sacred writers conveyed in the biblical writings. An alternative term might be *spiration* rather than *inspiration*, emphasizing the divine source and initiative rather than human genius or creativity. "In short," observes Carl F.H. Henry, "the Bible's life-breath as a literary deposit is divine."[2] While recognizing these shortcomings of the term *inspiration*, we will continue to use the word primarily because of its long-term standing in theological literature. The point that must be stressed when using this term is that it points to God as the source of Scripture.

It has been suggested that 2 Timothy 3:16 does not refer to all of Scripture because of the possible translation "Every Scripture inspired of God is also profitable" (ASV).[3] I. Howard Marshall has noted that this suggestion can be confidently rejected, since no New Testament author would have conceived of the possibility of a book's being classified as Scripture yet not inspired by God.[4] Some disagree with such an assertion and affirm a limited inspiration for the so-called salvific parts. Therefore, one cannot determine precisely what parts of the Bible are inspired. This viewpoint builds on a functional understanding of 2 Timothy 3:16. Such a translation, however, is highly unlikely because it makes the word translated *also (kai)* quite awkward. It is extremely doubtful that Scripture has a second characteristic ("also") before affirming its initial characteristic. The grammatical construction calls for much more straightforward translation: "The whole of Scripture is inspired and is ..." (KJV, NASB, CSB).[5] *Scripture* must refer to every passage of Scripture.[6] The grammatical significance of this understanding of "All Scripture is inspired" is not disputable.[7]

We must acknowledge that 2 Timothy 3:16 refers primarily to the Old Testament writings (*graphe*). Fifty occurrences of *graphe* (*Scripture*) are found in the New Testament, all of which refer primarily to the Old Testament, though the entirety of canonical Scripture is not ruled out. Furthermore, it is not too much to affirm that the construction used in verse 16 has a broader meaning that allows for the New Testament writings, as well. The grammatical construction "all Scripture" (*pas graphe*) can have a characteristic idea. The phrase would then carry the meaning "all that has the characteristics of canonical Scripture." Certainly, because of the normal usage of the term *Scripture* (*graphe*), plus the reference to the Holy Scriptures in verse 15, verse 16 primarily has the Old Testament in view. But since the phrase refers to the New Testament in 2 Peter 3:16, we can rightly suggest that at least the implication of the passage is that everything that takes on the character of Scripture is inspired. If that is the case, it is highly improbable that the apostle was making a distinction in his mind between the Greek and Hebrew texts of the Old Testament.[8] Thus, all translations that take on the characteristics of canonical Scripture can be described as inspired or at least virtually inspired.

The Inspired Word: Divine-Human Authorship

The passage in 2 Timothy 3 focuses primarily on the product of inspiration, while it includes the secondary aspects of the purpose and process. It asserts the activity of God throughout the entire process so that the completed, final product ultimately comes from Him. It is a mistake, however, to think of inspiration only in terms of the time when the Holy Spirit moved the human author to write. The biblical concept of inspiration allows for the activity in special ways in the process without requiring that we understand all of the Spirit's working in exactly the same way. Just as God providentially intervened in special ways for specific purposes in the processes of creation and preservation of the universe, alongside and within the superintending action of the Spirit to inspire human writings in the biblical books we can suggest a special work of the Spirit to bring God's revelation to the apostles and prophets.

God's Spirit was involved both in revealing specific messages to the prophets (see Jeremiah 1:1-9) and in guiding the authors of the historical sections in their research (see Luke 1:1-4). It is not outside the view of inspiration, then, to include the literary processes that take place on the human level behind Scripture. Summarizing the inclusiveness of inspiration, we can say, following Marshall, that it encompasses:

> ... the collection of information from witnesses, the use of written sources, the writing up and editing of such information, the composition of spontaneous letters, the committing to writing of prophetic messages, the collecting of the various documents together, and so on. At the same time, however, on the divine level we can assert that the Spirit, who moved on the face of the waters at creation (Genesis 1:2), was active in the whole process, so that the Bible can be regarded as both the words of men and the Word of God.[9]

This approach to inspiration seeks to take seriously the human factors, as well as the divine authorship, in the composition of the Bible. As we briefly noted in the previous chapter, the activity of the Holy Spirit with the activities of the human writers, through which the Bible was written, is called concursive inspiration. This affirmation of inspiration avoids any hint that God mechanically dictated the words of Scripture to the human authors so that they had no real part in Scripture's composition. Contrary to a view of mechanical dictation, our approach to inspiration attempts to take seriously the circumstances of the human authors.

The concursive approach allows for a viewpoint that gladly confesses that God's purpose is accomplished through the writer, but the emphasis of the Spirit's work is on the product of inspiration (the inscripturated word). We can assert that inspiration extends to the choice of words, based on a comprehensive, encompassing approach. This is accomplished by the Spirit's leading of the human author in points of research, reflection, and subsequent writing. It is possible that revelation and inspiration happened simultaneously at certain points in Scripture, such as the Ten Commandments and perhaps some apocalyptic visions like those in Ezekiel, Daniel, or Revelation.

Some might respond that we have contradicted ourselves by allowing for such direct inspiration at certain points or by assuring that inspiration extends even to the very words of Scripture, while simultaneously allowing for genuine human authorship. On the contrary, we believe that the answer is found in the spiritual characteristics of the biblical writers. These men of God had known God, had learned from Him, and had walked with Him in their spiritual pilgrimages for many years. God had prepared them through their familial, social, educational, and spiritual backgrounds for the task of inscripturating His word. The experiences of Moses, David, Jeremiah, Paul, Luke, and Peter differ; yet throughout their lives God was working to prepare and shape them and their vocabulary to pen the Scriptures. Beyond this we dare not say much about the *how* of inspiration, except to affirm God's providential superintendence of the entire process of inspiration.[10] It is quite plausible to suggest that just as revelation came in various ways (Hebrews 1:1-2), the process of inspiration differed with each author.

The process of inspiration may differ within passages and types of literature, but the quality of inspiration is the same throughout. This does not mean that some parts are more inspired than others; but the appearance of the result of inspiration is different among Luke's

Gospel, the Proverbs, the Apocalypse, and the Ten Commandments. God is the source of all Scripture, and His purposes are accomplished efficaciously. This means that the Sermon on the Mount or the Epistle to the Romans may be more readily recognized as inspired Scripture than the historical accounts in Kings or Chronicles. Yet this is due in part to the subject matter. The inspiration in such historical passages ensures the general chacteristic of reliability for these accounts. Even when the process of inspiration differs and is somehow less recognizable to the reader in some places, the entire Bible (all canonical Scripture = *pas graphe*) can be characterized as inspired (*theopneustos*).

The Inspired Word: Explanations of Inspiration

We would not naively maintain that the Bible fell from heaven on a parachute, inscribed with a peculiar heavenly language that uniquely suited it as an instrument for divine revelation. Nor would we claim that the Bible was dictated directly and immediately by God without reference to any local style or perspective. The presence of a multiplicity of historical, contextual, linguistic, and cultural factors must be maintained and accounted for.[11]

A number of views have developed in recent years that attempt to account for the divine-human character of inspired Scripture. A brief survey of these attempts will prove helpful for our discussion. Many of the contemporary theories attempt to deal seriously with the two-sided character of Scripture and also to explain how a book penned 2,000 years ago should be understood in a post-Enlightenment era.

The Enlightenment was a watershed in the history of Western civilization, a time when the Christian consensus was broken by a radical, secular spirit. The Enlightenment philosophy stressed the primacy of nature, a high view of reason and a low view of sin, and an antisupernatural bias; and it encouraged revolt against the traditional understanding of authority. Initiated by Friedrich Schleiermacher's *On Religion: Speeches to Its Cultured Despisers* at the turn on the 19th century, this philosophy was foundational for much of the liberal theology that dominated 19th-century European and early 20th-century

American thought. The contemporary assaults on classical foundations of scriptural inspiration and authority can be traced to pre-Enlightenment attacks on the Bible.[12] The positive element that has resulted from the questions raised by post-Enlightenment scholars has been a more careful consideration of the human authorship and historical context of Scripture. In the following survey, the dictation view has basically ignored the Enlightenment; the illumination view has surrendered to the Enlightenment; and in assorted ways the encounter, dynamic, and plenary views have attempted to respond to the Enlightenment while still maintaining the church's confession that the Bible is the Word of God. We will now examine these and other important models of inspiration.

The Dictation View

The dictation theory emphasized God's actual dictation of His word to the human writers. The theory develops from the passages, found primarily in the writings of the Old Testament prophets, in which the Spirit is pictured as telling the writer what to communicate. This view applies a proper assessment of particular aspects of Scripture ("Thus says the Lord") to the whole Bible but fails to consider seriously the distinctive styles of the different authors or the particular contexts they addressed.

Although it is right that the prophets claimed to hear God addressing them and then proclaimed His Word, this is not always parallel with the way other writers depicted themselves. For example, Luke told his readers that other people before him had attempted to write the story of Jesus and that he consulted these works and did additional research before compiling his Gospel (see Luke 1:1-4). Thus, the dictation theory cannot account for all aspects of Scripture. The dictation approach is without doubt confessed, perhaps unconsciously so, by numerous faithful believers. Therefore, it is often assumed that advocates of a plenary view (full or complete inspiration) hold to the dictation view, but adherents of the plenary view take great pains to dissociate themselves from the dictation theorists. It is right to judge the dictation theory as denying the humanness of the Bible and, therefore, as less than orthodox.[13]

The Illumination View

The illumination view maintains little more than the Spirit's working within the human authors to raise their religious insight and to enable them to express themselves with eloquent language. In this view, inspiration is the illumination of the authors beyond their normal abilities to express themselves creatively as men of human genius. Inspiration is very limited when understood in this manner, in relation not only to the nature of inspiration but also to the extent of inspiration. Portions of Scripture, such as poetry, proverbs, and parables, best exemplify this type of literary or religious insight. However, this approach fails to explain the inspiration of the entire Bible.[14]

The Encounter View

This view contends that the biblical writings only apparently or secondarily present descriptive statements about God and humankind. The view focuses on the reader's encounter with the biblical text so the reader will perceive the existential possibilities of human beings projected through it.[15]

The Neoorthodox View

Inspiration is perceived as an ongoing work of the Spirit through which the Bible becomes a means of revelation to specific individuals or communities. This approach stresses the idea of ongoing inspiration more than the Spirit's work at the time of the Bible's composition.

Inspiration brings the Bible to the contemporary human situation as a source of God's revelation. It is in this way that Karl Barth attempted to take seriously the human authorship of Scripture and the Bible as the Word of God. He tried to avoid a concept of inspiration that in some way confines the Holy Spirit to the Bible. It was a misunderstanding on his part, however, to assume that those who hold that the Bible was Spirit-inspired in its original composition ignore the Spirit's illumination of the text, thereby bringing it to life for present-day readers. Barth's stress on ongoing inspiration seems to ignore inspiration at the time of the Bible's composition. This view seems to make it possible for God's word to be encountered through Scripture.[16]

This view is inadequate, however, to account for the human and divine aspects of inscripturation. In comparison to the illumination theory, the encounter view, and the more radical views, this approach has many strengths and much to admire; yet it does not fully explain why we should trust the Bible as Barth did.

The Feminist View

This approach to Scripture has developed in the past few decades. It begins with an acknowledgement that the Bible has been written, translated, canonized, and interpreted by males. An ongoing process of inspiration, illumination, and exegetical reconstruction allows women to enter the center stage that they occupied during the days of Jesus' ministry.[17]

Liberation/Process Views

These radical views de-emphasize the divine nature of Scripture and stress an elevation of the human aspect. These theologies are diverse and difficult, if not impossible, to characterize. Generally, inspiration, authority, and interpretation are commingled and bound together. The Bible is viewed from a perspective of suspicion rather than of trust.[18]

The Dynamic or Sacramentalist View

This widely held approach endeavors to be a *via media*, a go-between, in contradistinction to the liberal and fundamentalist camps, emphasizing the combination of divine and human elements in the process of inspiration. Several important Baptist theologians, such as A.H. Strong and E.Y. Mullins, have advocated this view. G.C. Berkover, Donald Bloesch, and Paul Achtemeier have given this perspective a sacramentalist interpretation, which sees Scripture as a means of conveying God's grace. Contemporary explanations, such as William Abraham's, have expanded the view beyond the human author to see the role of the early Christian community in the composition of Scripture.

In many ways this approach originated as a reaction to the dictation view. It has been held by persons with diverse theological positions. In part it sees the work of the Spirit in directing the writer to the concepts he should have and then in allowing great freedom for the human author to express this idea in his own style through his own personality in a way consistent with and characteristic of his own situation and context.

The dynamic view's strength is its attempt to maintain the two-sided character of Scripture. Its stress on the creativity of the human author and his community is quite commendable. Inspiration, however, refers to the entire process, not just the momentary event of initiation. In some ways, similar to the neoorthodox view, inspiration and illumination are confused. The theory properly stresses the relation of inspiration to concepts, but it fails to account for the relationship between ideas and words. In emphasizing the process of inspiration, it does not place the emphasis where Scripture itself places it—on the product of inspiration. The real shortcoming of this approach, with its various nuances, is its imbalanced stress on God's initiating impulse rather than on His superintending work over the entire process and product. Finally, it must be seen that in this approach the emphasis is more on the biblical writers (who, granted, are referred to in 2 Peter 1:19-21) than on the writings, which is the emphasis of 2 Timothy 3:16.[19]

The Plenary View

The last view has been described in the first part of this chapter. We think that this approach best fits the biblical material. It carefully balances the Holy Spirit's influence on both the writers and (primarily) the writings. Inspiration is understood to extend to all portions of Holy Scripture (thus the adjective *plenary*), even beyond the direction of thoughts to the selection of words. Even though the words were those that God wanted communicated, the human writer's expression of this message evidences the situation of the writing and the author's unique style, background, and personality. We must recognize the element of mystery involved in this process, which does not fully explain the *how* of inspiration.

This approach seeks to do justice to the human factors in the Bible's composition and avoids any attempt to suggest that entire books of the Bible were dictated. We believe that this view, considered in the light of Baptist heritage and the classical Christian tradition, best accounts for the divine character of Scripture and the human circumstances of the Bible's composition.

Conclusion

Our method in this chapter might appear circular; but, as noted earlier, it is a viable, not a vicious, circle. We have explored the Bible's message to affirm its own inspiration and divine character. But when our model was evaluated and compared with other evidence and other models, it was seen to account best for the Bible's own claim and to balance the divine-human authorship of Scripture.

We recognize that inspiration preserves revelation. We acknowledge Scripture's literary diversity and affirm that it is more than a historical accident or decorative device. This recognition of literary diversity brings a healthy realization of the divine-human authorship of the Bible. Inspiration is thus concursive, including the human and divine aspects, and plenary, meaning that all Scripture is inspired. We affirm verbal inspiration, meaning that the Spirit's work influences even the choices of words by the human authors, while remaining cognizant of contemporary linguistic theory that suggests that meaning is at the sentence level and beyond. We believe that the essence or quality of inspiration is the same throughout Scripture, but it functions differently with the various kinds of literature in Scripture.[20] The issue that we must now address is the result of inspiration. Does plenary inspiration imply the truthfulness and dependability of Scripture? To these issues and questions we now turn our attention.

Endnotes

[1]See Millard J. Erickson, *Christian Theology*, 3 vols. (Grand Rapids: Baker Book House, 1983-86), 1:199-220. Large sections of this chapter are

taken from David S. Dockery, "The Divine-Human Authorship of Inspired Scripture," *Authority and Interpretation: A Baptist Perspective*, ed. Duane A. Garrett and Richard R. Melick, Jr. (Grand Rapids: Baker Book House, 1987), 13-43.

[2]Carl F.H. Henry, "The Authority and Inspiration of the Bible," The *Expositor's Bible Commentary*, ed. Frank E. Gaebelein, 12 vols. (Grand Rapids: Zondervan Publishing House, 1979), 1:13. Also see J.N.D. Kelley, *A Commentary on the Pastoral Epistles* (New York: Harper and Row, Publishers, Inc., 1963), 203.

[3]*American Standard Version*, copyright © 1901, Thomas Nelson & Sons, copyright © 1929, International Council of Religious Education.

[4]I. Howard Marshall, *Biblical Inspiration* (Grand Rapids: William B. Eerdmans Publishing Company, 1982), 25.

[5]C.F.D. Moule, *An Idiom Book of New Testament Greek* (Cambridge: University Press, 1953), 95.

[6]Gottlob Schrenk, "Grapho," *Theological Dictionary of the New Testament*, ed. Gerhard Kittel, 10 vols. (Grand Rapids: William B. Eerdmans Publishing Company, 1964). 1:759.

[7]Herman Ridderbos, *Studies in Scripture and Its Authority* (Grand Rapids: William B. Eerdmans Publishing Company, 1978), 24.

[8]Marshall, *Biblical Inspiration*, 43.

[9]Ibid., 42.

[10]Erickson, *Christian Theology*, 215-20. Also see B.B. Warfield, *The Inspiration and Authority of the Bible* (Philadelphia: Presbyterian and Reformed Publishing Company, 1948), 155-56.

[11]R.C. Sproul, *Knowing Scripture* (Downers Grove: InterVarsity Press, 1977), 101-11.

[12]See Bruce Demarest, "The Bible in the Enlightenment Era," *Challenges to Inerrancy*, ed. Gordon R. Lewis and Bruce Demarest (Chicago: Moody Press, 1984), 11-47; Colin Gunton, *Enlightenment and Alienation* (Grand Rapids: William B. Eerdmans Publishing Company, 1985), 111-52; Helmut Thielicke, *The Evangelical Faith*, trans. and ed. Geoffrey W. Bromiley, 3 vols. (Grand Rapids: William B. Eerdmans Publishing Company, 1974), 1:38-63; Bernard Ramm, *After Fundamentalism* (San

Francisco: Harper and Row, Publishers, Inc., 1983), who have attempted to articulate a post-Enlightenment/evangelical doctrine of Scripture.

[13] See John R. Rice, *Our God-Breathed Book, the Bible* (Murfreesboro, Tennessee: Sword of the Lord Press, 1969).

[14] See L.H. DeWolf, *A Theology of the Living Church* (New York: Harper and Row, Publishers, Inc., 1960), 48-75.

[15] See Rudolf Bultmann, *Kerygma and Myth: A Theological Debate*, ed. H.W. Bartsch (London: SCM Press, 1953).

[16] See Karl Barth, *Church Dogmatics*, trans. Geoffrey W. Bromiley and ed. T.F. Torrance, 4 vols. (Edinburgh: T&T Clark, 1956), 1:1, 52-335. Also see R.P.C. Hanson and A.T. Hanson, *The Bible Without Illusions* (London: SCM Press, 1989).

[17] Broadly speaking, we can identify three feminist perspectives: (1) rejectionist or post-Christian, (2) reformist or liberation, and (3) loyalist or evangelical. See Letty Russell, ed., *Feminist Interpretation of the Bible* (Philadelphia: Westminster Press, 1975).

[18] See Jose Misquez Bonino, *Doing Theology in a Revolutionary Situation* (Philadelphia: Fortress Press, 1975).

[19] See Augustus Hopkins Strong, *Systematic Theology* (Old Tappan, New Jersey: Fleming H. Revell Company, 1907), 211-22; W.T. Conner, *Christian Doctrine* (Nashville: Broadman, 1937), 27-43; James Leo Garrett, Jr., *Systematic Theology*, vol. 1 (Grand Rapids: Williams B. Eerdmans Publishing Company, 1990), 110-19.

[20] It seems possible that other words and sentences might have easily expressed God's truth if another writer in another context had written that portion of Scripture. See the classic article by W. Sanday, "The Psychology of Inspiration," *Dictionary of the Apostolic Church*, ed. James Hastings, vol. 1 (Grand Rapids: Baker Book House, 1973), 612-17.

CHAPTER 6

The Truthfulness and Dependability of the Bible

Word Alert

Inerrancy—the idea that when all the facts are known, the Bible (in its autographs, that is, the original documents), properly interpreted in light of the culture and the means of communication that had developed by the time of its composition, is completely true in all that it affirms, to the degree of precision intended by the author's purpose, in all matters relating to God and His creation.

Normative Scripture—a term indicating that Scripture's power is not limited by temporal or contextual matters. It indicates that the message of Scripture has binding authority for the contemporary church.

Infallibility—the view that the Bible is incapable of error and cannot deceive or mislead. Some contemporary scholars want to apply the term *infallible* only to the message of the Bible to avoid the affirmation that the Bible is also truthful in matters relating to history, geography, and related matters. The meaning given to *infallible* in this chapter is consistent with the classical meaning of the term, not with the revised meaning of some contemporary scholars.

Harmonization—an attempt to rearrange historical materials

---

as they are presented in such books as Samuel, Kings, Chronicles, the Gospels, and Acts so that similar accounts present a unified meaning.

Hermeneutics—from the Greek word *hermeneuein*, meaning *to explain, to express, to translate,* or *to interpret*. Basically, the term refers to the theory of interpretation. Traditionally, hermeneutics has sought to establish the principles and methods needed to interpret written texts, particularly sacred texts.

Epistemological—that which is concerned with the possibility, nature, and conditions of human knowledge. Knowledge of God becomes a possibility for humans at God's initiative by grace through faith.

Slippery-slope arguments—a popular term suggesting that after one generation abandons an orthodox view of Scripture, succeeding generations will continue to abandon other important orthodox beliefs.

Correspondence view of truth—a theory maintaining that truth consists in some form of correspondence between one's belief and actual conditions in the world. Although Christian faith is deeply rooted in history, the correspondence of the Christian position as a whole to ultimate reality will be verified only by the return of Christ at the end of history.

Coherence view of truth—a theory holding that truth consists in coherence with other statements known to be true. The theological, ethical, and historical message of Scripture is known to be true because of the general, overall consistency of the biblical writings, even though this consistency is expressed in great variety.

What is the result of the Holy Spirit's inspiration? In what sense can we confess that Scripture, which evidences genuine human authorship written in time-related contexts, is truthful or normative? The issue of the Bible's truthfulness or inerrancy has been a source of contention among evangelical Christians for years. Hopefully, in this chapter we can clarify some of the issues in the debate. We will see that inerrancy cannot be discussed unless we first understand revelation and inspiration. Inerrancy is the corollary and result of our affirmations about a full view of inspiration. Let us look at the meaning of the Bible's truthfulness or inerrancy and various ways it has been explained.

The Truthfulness of the Bible: Normative Scripture

Before we can discuss the Bible's truthfulness, we need to examine the possibility of a normative Scripture. Is the Bible wholly descriptive? If so, does that mean that students of Scripture are little more than historians or antique keepers, who display the exhibits in the best possible way? We have seen nothing in our study to this point that would lead us to draw that conclusion. A wholly descriptive approach is unacceptable, lacking all the dynamics of the experience of the biblical authors and their communities of faith.[1]

Perhaps we should rephrase the question. Does any Bible student accept a descriptive approach completely? Is not the real issue to what extent the Bible is normative for the contemporary church? Even Rudolf Bultmann, while maintaining that first-century cultural patterns cannot be considered normative, nevertheless sought to reinterpret these patterns for the contemporary church.

Although the cultural background and environment have changed considerably since the biblical writings were penned, the human condition has not changed. The unity of the biblical message speaks in a normative character to the human condition, men and women created in the image of God yet fallen. We can make this confession for the following reasons:

1. The Scriptures are the result of divine inspiration.

2. They proclaim the saving acts of God.
3. They were written near the time of the saving acts of God.
4. They are based on the prophetic-apostolic authority.

Even with cultural advancement and scientific progress, the need of men and women for a right standing and a right relationship with God remains unchanged. The reason is that even the advancing wisdom and knowledge of the world cannot help humanity in the ultimate aspect of life (see 1 Corinthians 1-4). The basic problem of how sinful human beings are to approach a holy God and how these persons are to live in relationship to the life-giving Spirit of God is the same for all ages.

Therefore, the purpose of divinely inspired teaching about God and about matters relating to the acts and purposes of God is normative for the contemporary church. When such matters are proclaimed and confessed in the 20th century, however, mere repetition of early Christian beliefs may not be sufficient; a restatement that awakens modern readers to an awareness that the Bible speaks in relevant ways to contemporary issues in church and society is also necessary.[2] When Scripture is approached from this perspective, it is necessary to determine underlying principles for all Scripture that address the contemporary situation. This is necessary even if the direct teaching of Scripture is somewhat limited by cultural-temporal factors (see 1 Corinthians 16:20; Ephesians 6:5; 1 Timothy 5:23).

Believers recognize that this process of determining underlying principles is necessary because of the two-sided character of Scripture. Because it is authored by human beings in specific contexts, certain passages may be contextually limited; but because they are divinely inspired, the underlying principles are normative and applicable for the church in every age. When approaching the Bible, in recognition of its authoritative and normative character, we can discover truth[3] and its ramification for the answers to life's ultimate questions, as well as guidelines and principles for godly living in the contemporary world.[4]

The Truthfulness of the Bible: Baptist Confessions

We have indicated the importance of a normative Scripture. Now we must probe further and ask if we can also confess the truthfulness and reliability of Scripture. This is a very important matter, not because it is necessary for salvation but because it is important to maintain an orthodox and biblical confession of salvation and other essential doctrines as well.

Inerrancy is a "red-flag" word for many Christians. The word sometimes seems to promise too much. Other times it is claimed that the historical clarifications used in the discussion of inerrancy, in effect, denature the doctrine. Misunderstanding of the concept abounds.

As Christians have disagreed about matters of biblical inspiration, authority, and interpretation, a doctrinal foundation to evaluate such issues has often been absent. Even men and women who believed biblical stories as reported, who affirmed the historical foundation of Holy Scripture, and who never for one minute doubted the miraculous claims of the Bible have been confused by the use of such terms as *inerrant* and *infallible*. In light of this confusion, it will be helpful to understand how the concepts of truthfulness, infallibility, and inerrancy have been used by Baptists across the years.

Baptists have published numerous confessions of faith since the early years of the 17th century. We will examine the statements about Holy Scripture in representative Baptist confessions.[5]

Article 23 of Thomas Helwys' Confession (1611) sets forth the following view of Scripture:

> That the scriptures off the Old and New Testament are written for our instruction, 2 Tim. 3:16 and that wee ought to search them for they testifie off CHRIST, Io. [John] 5:30. And therefore to be vsed with all reverence, as conteyning the Holie Word off God, which onelie is our direction in al thinges whatsoever.

The First London Confession (1644), a Calvinistic Baptist confession that predates the Westminster Confession, states in article 7:

> The Rule of this Knowledge, Faith, and Obedience, concerning
> the worship and service of God, and all other Christian duties,
> is not man's inventions, opinions, devices, lawes, constitutions,
> or traditions unwritten whatsoever, but onely the word of God
> contained in the Canonicall Scriptures.

The Second London Confession (1677, 1689), basically following
the wording and emphases of the Westminster Confession, contains
10 articles on the Scriptures. In addition to articles on the canon (2), a
denial of the authority of the Apocrypha (3), statements on illumination
(6), the original languages (8), and the perspicuity of Scripture in regard
to salvation (7), it affirms:

1. The Holy Scripture is the only sufficient, certain,
   and infallible rule of all saving Knowledge, Faith,
   and Obedience.
2. The Authority of the Holy Scripture for which it ought
   to be believed dependeth not upon the testimony of any
   man, or Church; but wholly upon God (who is truth it
   self) the Author thereof; therefore it is to be received,
   because it is the Word of God.
3. We may be moved and induced by the testimony of the
   Church of God, to an high and reverent esteem of the
   Holy Scriptures ... it doth abundantly evidence it self
   to be the Word of God; yet, not withstanding; our full
   perswasion, and assurance of the infallible truth, and
   divine authority thereof, is from the inward work of the
   Holy Spirit, bearing witness by and with the Word in
   our Hearts.

The Philadelphia Confession (1742), which so greatly influenced
Baptists in America, followed the Second London Confession. At

no place was the Philadelphia statement more influential than in Charleston, where the theological formation of Southern Baptist leaders Richard Furman, J.P. Boyce, and Basil Manly, among others, took place.

The New Hampshire Confession (1833), an altogether new document for Baptists in America, articulates a high view of Scripture with language that has been officially adopted by many Baptist bodies. Article 1 declares:

> We believe [that] the Holy Bible was written by men divinely inspired, and is a perfect treasure of heavenly instruction; that it has God for its author, salvation for its end, and truth, without any mixture of error, for its matter; that it reveals the principles by which God will judge us; and therefore is, and shall remain to the end of the world, the true centre of Christian union, and the supreme standard by which all human conduct, creeds, and opinions should be tried.

The Baptist Faith and Message (1925, 1963) basically adopted the wording of the New Hampshire Confession, with minor changes. The 1925 statement, edited by E.Y. Mullins, inserted the adjective *religious* to modify the word *opinions*. The 1963 confession, edited by Herschel H. Hobbs, added the phrase "and is the record of God's revelation of Himself to man." A hermeneutical guide was also provided: "The criterion by which the Bible is to be interpreted is Jesus Christ." The 2000 version of the Baptist Faith and Message emphasized that "all Scripture is totally true and trustworthy. It reveals the principles by which God judges us, and therefore is, and will remain to the end of the world, the true center of Christian union, and the supreme standard by which all human conduct, creeds, and religious opinions should be tried. All Scripture is a testimony to Christ, who is Himself the focus of divine revelation."

Readily apparent in these statements is the confidence that Baptists have had in the Bible, its inspiration, truthfulness, and authority. The Bible is "written for our instruction," and it "testifies of Christ"; "it is the infallible rule of saving knowledge, faith, and obedience." We have this confidence because "of the Holy Spirit, bearing witness by and with the Word in our hearts." Thus, we know that it is "divinely inspired and is a perfect treasure of heavenly instruction" and that it has "God for its author, salvation for its end, and truth, without any mixture of error, for its matter." The nuances and distinctions are worthy of notation, but all of the statements demonstrate a commitment to the Bible's total truthfulness and complete dependability.

The Truthfulness of the Bible: Views of Inerrancy

We have seen the confidence that Baptists have expressed in the written Word of God. But this general confidence has been articulated in various ways. It will be instructive for us at this important juncture in our study to survey different approaches to this subject. The name of a Baptist who represents each position will also be given.

1. *Naive inerrancy* assumes that God actually dictated the Bible to the writers. The passages that indicate that the Spirit told the author precisely what to write are regarded as typical of the entire Bible. It seemingly ignores style differences and historical and cultural contexts. An example of this approach can be found in John R. Rice, *Our God-Breathed Book, the Bible* (Murfreesboro, TN: Sword of The Lord Press, 1969).

2. *Absolute inerrancy* affirms that the Bible is accurate and true in all matters and that the writers intend to give a considerable amount of exact data in such matters. This view tries to separate itself from the view of mechanical dictation but sometimes fails to take seriously the human aspect of Scripture and its historical contexts. Representation of this view is the famous work by Harold Lindsell, *The Battle for the Bible* (Grand Rapids: Zondervan Publishing House, 1976).

3. *Balanced inerrancy* affirms that the Bible is completely true in all the Bible affirms, to the degree of precision intended by the writer. This position regards scientific matters as phenomenal; that is, they are often reported as they appeared to the human writer, which perhaps may be different from the way they really are (see the section "The Phenomena of Scripture" in chapter 4). It regards the historical matters as accurate, though sometimes in a very general way. This approach attempts to take seriously the human and divine aspects of inscripturation. Articulations of this view can be found in Millard J. Erickson, *Christian Theology*, volume 1 (Grand Rapids: Baker Book House, 1983), and in Carl F.H. Henry, *God, Revelation, and Authority*, volume 4 (Waco: Word Books, 1981).

4. *Limited inerrancy* maintains that the Bible is inerrant in matters of salvation and ethics or faith and practice. Inspiration did not necessarily protect the biblical writers from misstatements in matters of science or history (empirical areas). This, however, is no problem, because the Bible is inerrant in the matters for which the Bible was given. This highly nuanced view can be found in Clark H. Pinnock, *The Scripture Principle* (San Francisco: Harper and Row, Publishers, Inc., 1984).

5. *Functional inerrancy* contends that the Bible inerrantly accomplishes its purposes. This view does not equate inerrancy with factuality. The purpose of the Bible is to reveal God and to bring people into fellowship with Him. To the degree that this is done, the Bible can be said to be inerrant. Often this pragmatic approach sees the whole discussion as distracting and irrelevant. Exemplary of this view is an article by David M. Scholer, "The Nature of Biblical Authority: A Moderate Perspective,"

Conservative, Moderate, Liberal: The Bible Authority Debate,
ed. Charles R. Blaisdell (St. Louis: CBP Press, 1990).

6. *Errant but authoritative* is a view built on an encounter
   view of inspiration. It sees the Bible not as revelation but
   as a pointer to a personal encounter with God. Questions
   of truth or falseness are of little concern. It reaches the
   faulty conclusion that the Bible contains errors because it
   was written by human beings who are sinful and therefore
   err. The presence of errors in no way militates against
   the functional purpose of authority of the Bible when
   God is encountered through the reading of it. This view,
   at least in large measure, is an existential view of truth.
   Representing this view is Charles W. Allen, "The Nature
   of Biblical Authority: A Liberal Response," *Conservative,
   Moderate, Liberal: The Biblical Authority Debate,* ed. Charles
   R. Blaisdell (St. Louis: CBP Press, 1990).

These views occasionally overlap; but generally, we can evaluate them
in terms of their faithfulness to the doctrine of special revelation, plenary
inspiration, and the Bible's divine-human authorship. View 1 (naive
inerrancy) reflects a Docetic tendency that de-emphasizes the human
nature of Scripture. View 6 (errant but authoritative) de-emphasizes
the divine nature of Scripture and, like view 1, should be seen outside
the parameters of the classical Christian tradition.

The other four views are similar; yet each has its own emphasis. View
2 (absolute inerrancy) sometimes builds too much on a correspondence
view of truth and resulting harmonizations (a view that biblical material
must correspond with verifiable facts outside the biblical record). The
emphasis on accuracy or precision sometimes leads the reader to run
roughshod over the historical context of Scripture, forcing it to say
what it does not say. Views 4 and 5 fall into the trap of viewing the
Bible pragmatically. Among their many strengths is an emphasis on
the redemptive nature and emphasis of Scripture, but they sometimes

fail to see the importance of the Bible's faithful historical foundation.

Views 2, 3, 4, and 5 all attempt to affirm the Bible as God's Word, inspired by the Holy Spirit and written by human authors. View 3 (balanced inerrancy), however, is more faithful to our previous findings about the nature of revelation and inspiration. This position stresses that what the Bible affirms is completely true, employing both a coherence view (a view that biblical truth is verified within the biblical revelation in a coherent manner) and a correspondence view of truth at appropriate places. It attempts to be sensitive to the diversity and development in Holy Scripture, recognizing different types of literature, while seeking to determine the original meaning of Scripture. Harmonization is accepted as a legitimate means of handling the diversity in the biblical text, though never at the expense of making the Bible say what it does not say. Because the Bible is a divine-human Book, the interpretive tools of literary and historical criticism are employed with care and faith-oriented presuppositions. We will focus our attention on further definition and clarification of this viewpoint.

The Truthfulness of the Bible: Dependability Affirmed

Misunderstandings about this affirmation have resulted from false associations with a literalistic hermeneutic or with dictation theories of inspiration. Additional problems have developed from careless statements on the part of advocates who have been overzealous in their defense of the doctrine or who have concentrated unduly on issues of errors when the focus should instead be placed on truthfulness and falseness.

This affirmation is important primarily for theological and epistemological reasons. Shifting the argument to issues of salvation only confuses the issue. As stated earlier, individual salvation does not depend on one's confession of inerrancy, but consistent theological method and instruction need the base of inerrancy to maintain an orthodox confession of Christian truth. Thus, we see that biblical inerrancy or truthfulness goes hand in hand with inspiration as the foundation on which other theological building blocks are laid.

With these warnings behind us and an awareness of the complexity of the issue, we wish to offer a definition of *inerrancy*.[6] *Inerrancy* means that when all the facts are known, the Bible (in its autographs, that is, the original documents), properly interpreted in light of the culture and the means of communication that had developed by the time of its composition, is completely true in all that it affirms, to the degree of precision intended by the author's purpose, in all matters relating to God and His creation.

No doubt, some will say that with the carefulness of the definition, which tries to recognize the complexity of the issue, it is futile to carry on further discussion. But hopefully, the exact opposite is true. The definition seeks to be faithful to the phenomena of Scripture, as well as to theological affirmations in Scripture about the veracity of God. It will be helpful at this point to offer some brief comments about the definition.

When all the facts are known. The statement begins from the vantage point of faith, recognizing that we may not have all the data necessary on this side of eternity that applies to the Bible. It is also likely that our sinful, finite minds may misinterpret a fact. This does not imply that salvific faith or confidence in the Scriptures is a blind leap into the darkness. It is faith enabled by the Holy Spirit. The Spirit's witness confirms these truths to our hearts at this time, even though they are not presently evident to us physically.

The Bible. Inerrancy applies to all aspects of the Bible as originally written. A claim to complete inerrancy is limited to the original words of the biblical text, not applying to the text itself. In other words, a reference to the autographs is not restricted to some lost codex but affirms the original words that were written by the prophetic-apostolic messengers. Our confession of inerrancy and inspiration applies also to translations to the degree that they represent accurately the original words. We believe that we can express great confidence in our present translations. Therefore, the appeal to autographs is not intended as an apologetic side step but is a theological appeal to the providence and veracity of God in His superintending work of inspiration. The appeal to the autographs is never intended to remove trust in our present-day translations but to ensure and confirm faith in these translations, emphasizing that they rest on a sure foundation.

Properly interpreted. The definition recognizes that statements about the nature of the text cannot be separated from hermeneutical issues.[7] Before falseness can be recognized, it is necessary to know whether a text has been interpreted properly. Matters of precision and accuracy must be judged in light of culture and means of communication that had developed by the time of the text's composition and in view of the author's overall purpose. Biblical interpretation must take into account the context, background, culture, literary genre, and purpose of the writing.

Is completely true. A very important aspect of the definition is the evaluation of inerrancy in terms of truthfulness and falseness rather than precision or error. This separates the issue from grammatical mistakes or a lack of precision in reports. Inerrancy, on one hand, must not be associated with strict tests of precision in which careless harmonization attempts to bring about a precision uncommon to the text itself.[8] On the other hand, it is not helpful to dilute the concept of inerrancy by saying that it means that the biblical writers were not guilty of "willful deceit."[9] Recognizing that the issue is truthfulness confirms what many have implied when declaring *inerrancy* an improper term to describe Scripture. We prefer the terms *truthfulness* and *dependability*; but *inerrancy*, like *inspiration*, is deeply imbedded in theological literature. Also, words like *reliable, dependable,* and *truthful* are sometimes used by persons who deny inerrancy. It is therefore best to emphasize careful definitions rather than to change terms. Although not popularized until the past decade, the affirmation of *inerrancy* is also faithful to Baptist beliefs, as can be seen in the quotation by J.M. Frost in the preface of this book. (J.P. Boyce, John Broadus, Basil Manly, B.H. Carroll, A.T. Robertson, George Truett, and many other Baptist giants of the past and present have also made this claim.)

In all matters. The definition states that inerrancy is not limited merely to religious matters, thus creating, or at least providing the framework for, an improper dualism. Inerrancy applies to all areas of knowledge, since all truth is God's truth. Yet issues of history and science must be evaluated in light of the communicative mean at the time of inscripturation. Modern scientific thought and the concern of historiography for precision are not proper standards for first-century (and earlier) authors. These matters must be analyzed in light of the author's purpose and intended level of precision, which generally should be understood in terms of phenomenological observation.

Conclusion

The issue of biblical inerrancy is best understood as a claim to the Bible's truthfulness. In providing statements about a truthful Bible, we must be cautious with slippery-slope arguments or avoid them altogether. God can, and certainly does, overrule departure from orthodoxy, as church history bears testimony. Certainly, the Reformation itself witnesses to the truth of this claim. We must avoid unnecessary associations with a literalistic, stilted hermeneutic; but we should not dissociate the issue of truthfulness from hermeneutics. Inerrancy is a direct implication and an important corollary of a plenary, concursive view of inspiration, not necessarily a direct teaching of Scripture, although Matthew 5:18 and John 10:35 strongly seem to suggest that all Scripture is inerrant.

Our understanding of Scripture's truthfulness needs to be consistent with the divine-human nature of Scripture. This means that the fact of divine-human authorship must be accounted for and that Scripture's witness to itself and its divine inspiration must be satisfied. Such an approach is not primarily dependent on a correspondence view of truth (the view that biblical material must correspond with verifiable facts outside the biblical record). Although many affirmations of Scripture can be verified outside the biblical record, most theological and ethical statements lie outside the realm of verification. A coherence view of truth is more applicable for all Scripture (a view that biblical truth is verified within the biblical revelation in a coherent manner).

Our affirmation does not suggest an exhaustive knowledge of God or any other subject. Neither does it deny human authorship. It does not promise a correct interpretation of Scripture, nor does it guarantee an accurate preservation of Scripture so as to produce perfect translations. It sets certain limits on the range of acceptable answers in matters of biblical interpretation and criticism and provides a solid foundation for trustworthy translations of Scripture. As many orthodox theologians have observed, theology that is not built on a reliable view of Scripture operates within the circle of human concepts and experiences and has no reference point. A renewed commitment to the truthfulness and dependability of Scripture is the first step toward healing the deadly sickness in today's theological trends. We believe that the Bible is inspired and true. We joyfully and confidently commit our lives to its message and gladly proclaim this truth to others. How is this inspired, truthful, and dependable Scripture preserved? Our next chapter deals with this significant issue.

Endnotes

[1] See Donald Guthrie, *New Testament Theology* (Downers Grove: InterVarsity Press, 1981), 953-82.

[2] John Jefferson Davis, "Contextualization and the Nature of Theology," *The Necessity of Systematic Theology*, ed. John Jefferson Davis (Grand Rapids: Baker Book House, 1980), 169-85; Clark H. Pinnock, *The Scripture Principle* (San Francisco: Harper and Row, Publishers, Inc., 1984), 210-21; David Hesselgrave, "Contextualization and Revelation Epistemology," *Inerrancy and Hermeneutics*, ed. Earl D. Radmacher and R.D. Preus (Grand Rapids: Zondervan Publishing House, 1986), 693-764.

[3] Anthony C. Thiselton, "Truth," *The New International Dictionary of New Testament Theology*, ed. Colin Brown, 3 vols. (Grand Rapids: Zondervan Publishing House, 1978), 3:874-902.

[4] Anthony C. Thiselton, *The Two Horizons* (Grand Rapids: William B. Eerdmans Publishing Company, 1980), 432-38.

[5] Citations from the confessions are from William L. Lumpkin, *Baptist*

Confessions of Faith (Valley Forge: The Judson Press, 1959). Also see James Leo Garrett, Jr., "Biblical Authority According to Baptist Confessions of Faith," *Review and Expositor* 76 (1979), 43-54; "Sources of Authority in Baptist Thought," *Baptist History and Heritage* 13 (1978), 47-49.

[6]Very careful statements on the subject can be found in Millard J. Erickson, *Christian Theology*, 3 vols. (Grand Rapids: Baker Book House, 1983-86), 1:221-40. Paul D. Feinberg has written two helpful articles: "The Meaning of Inerrancy," *Inerrancy*, ed. Norman L. Geisler (Grand Rapids: Zondervan Publishing House, 1980), 267-304, and "Bible, Inerrancy and Infallibility of," *Evangelical Dictionary of Theology*, ed. W.A. Elwell (Grand Rapids: Baker Book House, 1984), 141-45. Two volumes that support the affirmations of this chapter are: D.A. Carson and John D. Woodbridge, eds., *Scripture and Truth* (Grand Rapids: Zondervan Publishing House, 1983), and Roger R. Nicole and J. Ramsey Michaels, eds., *Inerrancy and Common Sense* (Grand Rapids: Baker Book House, 1980).

[7]The most helpful work to date relating inspiration to interpretation is Clark H. Pinnock's *Scripture Principle* (San Francisco: Harper and Row, Publishers, Inc., 1984), especially pages 197-202.

[8]Harold Lindsell's undue concern for harmonization in *The Battle for the Bible* (Grand Rapids: Zondervan Publishing House, 1976), 174-76, makes this mistake.

[9]Jack B. Rogers and Donald McKim, *The Authority and Interpretation of the Bible: An* [sic] *Historical Approach* (San Francisco: Harper and Row, Publishers, Inc., 1979), 111, define their confession about the nature of Scripture in terms of a lack of willful deception.

CHAPTER 7

The Text and Canonicity of the Bible

Papyri fragments—writings on sheets that were formed by cutting the stems off an Egyptian plant into long, thin strips placed in two crosswise layers and glued together by hammer blows.

Vulgate—a Latin translation of the Bible by Jerome near the close of the fourth century A.D. It became the common version of the Catholic Church during the Middle Ages.

Marcionism—a movement in the early church based on the teachings of Marcion, a second-century heretic. Marcion rejected the Old Testament and issued his own New Testament consisting of an abbreviated Gospel of Luke and 10 Letters of Paul (excluding the Pastorals). Marcion set forth stark contrasts between the God of the Old Testament and the Christ of the New Testament.

Montanism—a prophetic movement or sect that developed in Phrygia in Asia Minor around A.D. 172. It emphasized an ecstatic manner of utterance that ran counter to the tradition of Israelite and Christian prophecy.

Muratorian Fragment—a fragmentary list of New Testament books known in Rome around A.D. 200. The list attests that the canonical books that were received in the church in the west were authorized to be read in public worship services. The list is named after L.A. Muratori, who discovered and published the document in the middle of the 18th century.

The subjects of translations and canonicity have been mentioned previously. In this chapter we will investigate the meanings of these terms. What was the process for determining the books in the canon? What tests were used in this process? How does this issue of canon relate to the unity and diversity of the Bible? We will examine these issues, and a short history of these matters will also be provided.

The Bible: The Transmission of God's Word

We are briefly informed of the transmission of the preexilic parts of the Old Testament. Deuteronomy 31:9-26 commands that "the book of the law" be placed by the side of the ark of the covenant and read publicly every seventh year at the Feast of Tabernacles. This directive points to an early form of preservation and transmission. The oracles of some of the prophets were committed to writing and entrusted for safekeeping until the prophecies should be fulfilled and the prophets vindicated (see Isaiah 8:16; Jeremiah 36).

It is testimony to the providence of God that so much Old Testament material survived the Babylonian exile. Psalms that figured prominently in preexilic worship remained unsung for two generations while the temple lay in ruins. Although the people could not sing the Lord's song in a foreign land (see Psalm 137:4), they did not forget the familiar words, which were later reincorporated into the postexilic psalter and celebrated in the second temple.

Important examples of the transmission of the writings in the postexilic period are Ezra's mission to Jerusalem with the law of God in his hand (see Ezra 7:14) and the public reading of "the book of the law of Moses" in Jerusalem during the Feast of Tabernacles in what was probably the initial year of Nehemiah's governorship (see Nehemiah 8:1-18). A critical threat to the transmission of the Scriptures came with the persecution under Antiochus IV (ca. 167 B.C.), when the officials burned "the books of the law" that were found. Jews who possessed these books were executed (1 Maccabees 1:56). The persecution lasted three years. But when it was over, copies of the Scriptures could be procured from Jewish communities outside Judea.

The New Testament documents were all written in Greek in the first century. Transmission of individual documents began prior to their corporate collection. Early in the second century the four Gospels and the Pauline Letters were circulated as two collections. From that time on, collections, rather than individual documents, were transmitted.

Acts and the General Epistles were generally associated together. The Book of Revelation, for the most part, was transmitted by itself.

The Bible: Early Attestations and Translations

The early copies of the Old Testament were written on leather or papyrus from the time of Moses to the time of Malachi. The Jews' mystical reverence for the sacred books prompted them to bury copies that had become too old for use. Providentially, these scrolls, known as the Dead Sea Scrolls, were discovered in 1947. Until that discovery we did not possess copies of the Old Testament dated earlier than A.D. 895.

The well-known Masoretic text was preserved by traditionalists, known as Masoretes. The Masoretes added accents and vowel points to the Hebrew text. They also devised extremely complex methods to safeguard the making of copies (ca. A.D. 600-950). They checked each copy carefully by counting from the middle letter of pages, books, and sections. Everything countable was counted by the Masoretes. When the Dead Sea Scrolls were discovered, they provided us an earlier Hebrew text dating from the second century B.C. This was true for all Old Testament books except Esther. These discoveries have confirmed the reliability of the older Masoretic texts.

Historical research and archaeological findings have led to the discovery of other important copies of translations of the Old Testament. These include the Samaritan Pentateuch; the Aramaic Targums; the Syriac version, called the Peshitta; and the Latin translation of Jerome (ca. A.D. 400), called the Vulgate. The most important of all the translations of the Old Testament is the pre-Christian Greek version called the Septuagint (LXX). Tradition claims that this version was produced by 72 Jewish elders at the request of Ptolemy II, king of Egypt, for the use of the Greek-speaking Jewish community in Alexandria, Egypt.

With rare exceptions the Septuagint manuscripts that have been passed down were copied and preserved by Christians, not by Jews. The translation is of unequal quality. The Pentateuch, as we would expect, was treated with special care. The Septuagint is frequently quoted in the New Testament, since it served as the Bible of Greek-speaking Christians in the apostolic period. Many of the important theological terms in the New Testament derive their meanings from their usage in the Septuagint.

While the Septuagint is not considered a completely trustworthy rendering of the Hebrew, it still permits us to compare the Greek with our Hebrew versions. The same can be said of the Targums, which are Aramaic paraphrases of Scripture, and of the Talmud, which records the comments of rabbis on the written text. All of these assure us of having a faithful text of the Old Testament.

Early translations of the New Testament include Latin, Syriac, and Coptic (an Egyptian translation). Transmission and translation of the New Testament text present different issues than of the Old Testament. There are more than 5,000 manuscripts of the New Testament, making the New Testament the best-attested document among all ancient writings. New Testament scholar F.F. Bruce has written:

> Perhaps we can appreciate how wealthy the New Testament is in manuscript attestation if we compare the textual material from other ancient historical works. For Caesar's *Gallic War* (composed between 58 and 56 B.C.) there are several extant MSS [manuscripts], but only nine or ten are good, and the oldest is some 900 years later than Caesar's day. Of the 142 books of the Roman History of Livy (59 B.C. – A.D. 17), only thirty-five survive; these are known to us from not more than twenty MSS of any consequence, only one of which, and that containing fragments of Books III-VI, is as old as the fourth century. Of the fourteen books of the *Histories* of Tacitus (c. A.D. 100) only four and a half survive; of the sixteen books of his Annals, ten survive in full and two in part. The text of these extant portions of his two great historical works depends entirely on two MSS, one of the ninth century and one of the eleventh. ... *The History of Thucydides* (c. 460-400 B.C.) is known to us from eight MSS, the earliest belonging

to c. A.D. 900, and a few papyrus scraps, belonging to about the beginning of the Christian era. The same is true of the *History of Herodotus* (c. 480-425 B.C.). Yet no classical scholar would listen to an argument that the authenticity of Herodotus or Thucydides is in doubt because the earliest MSS of their works which are of any use are over 1,300 years later than the originals.[1]

Not only are there many more copies of the New Testament, but many of them are also quite early. Approximately 75 papyri fragments can be dated from the early second to the mid-eighth century, covering 25 of the 27 New Testament books. In addition, hundreds of parchment copies survive, 2,000 church worship books containing many Scripture passages, and over 80,000 New Testament quotations or allusions in writings of the church fathers.

From these early copies and translations scholars have tried to recapture the original Greek text. The work has been successful, and today we possess a very accurate and reliable New Testament text. It is true that we do not have the first written texts of either the Old or the New Testament. But sufficient evidence exists that our English versions are trustworthy translations of reliable Hebrew and Greek texts, which faithfully represent the originals.[2]

The Bible: In the Language of the People

All ancient translations were called forth by practical needs. In addition to the Septuagint, there were other Greek versions of the Old Testament. Origen (ca. A.D. 185-254) produced a remarkable work called the *Hexapla*, in which he compared the Hebrew Bible with these Greek versions and his own revisions. The whole Bible existed in at least seven versions (Latin, Syriac, Coptic, Armenian, Georgian, Gothic, and Ethiopic) by the sixth century A.D.

The movement to translate the Bible into the language of the people found very little support during the Middle Ages. The Latin translation, known as the Vulgate, became the church's standard translation. At the time of the Reformation, through the impetus of Martin Luther, the needs of the people again brought about new translations. These movements occurred not only in Germany but also in France and England. Modern Bible societies have translated the Bible into the vernacular of people around the world, even Third World and tribal languages.

Today many versions of the Bible are available in English.[3] These versions can be classified in various ways. The *King James Version* (1611) is the most well-known of all English versions, but several English translations were completed prior to it. Two of the most important, in the last decades of the 14th century, were associated with the name John Wycliffe. In 1534 William Tyndale completed what was then the definitive English translation. Miles Coverdale published several editions of the English Bible called the Great Bible. Some months after James VI of Scotland became king of England as James I in 1603, he convened a conference to deal with various controversial issues in the church. From that meeting came the proposal to produce a fresh English translation from the Greek and Hebrew texts. Because of the king's sponsorship, the translation was named the *King James Version*.

Several significant translations have appeared in the 19th and 20th centuries, most of which are included in the following list. Comments on the most important of these will follow. In the middle column the first date indicates the year of publication of the first portion of the project; the second date indicates the year the project was completed.

Translation	Year	Translator
The Holy Bible	1833	Noah Webster
Literal Translation	1863	Robert Young
English Revised Version	1881-85	54 scholars
The Holy Scriptures	1871-90	John Nelson Darby
Twentieth-Century New Testament	1898	3 scholars, 32 laypersons

American Standard Version	1901	30 American scholars
The Emphasized Bible	1872-1902	Joseph B. Rotherham
New Testament in Modern Speech	1903	Richard E. Weymouth
The Bible: A New Translation	1913-24	James Moffatt
The Complete Bible, an American Translation	1923-35	E.J. Goodspeed and others
The New Testament: A Private Translation in the Language of the People	1937	Charles Williams
Revised Standard Version of the Bible	1949-52	32 scholars
The New Testament in Modern English	1958	J.B. Phillips
The Holy Bible: The Berkeley Version in Modern English	1959	Gemtt Verkuyl and others
The New World Translation of the Holy Scriptures	1950-60	New World Translation Committee
The New Testament: An Expanded Translation	1956-61	Kenneth S. Wuest
The New English Bible	1961	C.H. Dodd and others
The Amplified Bible	1958-65	Francis Siemert and others
The Jerusalem Bible	1966	28 Roman Catholic scholars
The Modern Language Bible	1969	3 scholars
The Barclay New Testament	1961-70	C.H. Dodd and 50 others

The New American Bible	1970	50 Roman Catholic scholars
New American Standard Bible	1963-71	58 scholars
The Living Bible, Paraphrased	1962-71	Kenneth Taylor
Good News Bible, The Bible in Today's English Version	1966-76	Robert G. Bratcher and others
The Holy Bible in the Language of Today: An American Translation	1976	William F. Beck
New International Version	1973-78	115 scholars (revised and updated in 2011)
New King James Version	1979-82	130 scholars
The Reader's Digest Bible	1982	Bruce Metzger and others
The Word: New Century Version, New Testament	1983-86	21 scholars
New Revised Standard Version	1990	Bruce Metzger and others
English Standard Version	2001	J.I. Packer and Wayne Grudem, editors
Christian Standard Bible	2017	More than 100 scholars from 17 denominations worked together on this project, led by Thomas Schreiner and David Allen

Several translations are attempts at literal, word-for-word equivalents. Examples are the *American Standard Version* and the *New American Standard Bible*. Increasingly, translators have felt the need to express the meaning of the original in the language of their times. Translators have therefore employed idiomatic English, seeking words or phrases that would communicate the range of meanings of words in the original sources. This approach, referred to as dynamic equivalence, is best seen in *The New English Bible* and the *New International Version*. The *Christian Standard Bible* has received strong affirmation for its approach that highlights precise translation and readability in contemporary English. Some translations are really paraphrases, which actually interpret the original source for the reader. The best examples of this expanded approach are *The Living Bible*, *The Amplified Bible*, and *The New Testament in Modern English*. Paraphrases are generally less reliable than translations, which seek to express the meaning of the original through more literal or dynamic-equivalent methods. For devotional purposes, paraphrases are excellent; but for serious study of the Bible, translations that faithfully represent the original sources are necessary.

How do we know which books to study or which books should be included in a Bible translation? The answers to these questions lie in a discussion of the biblical canon.

The Bible: Canonical Books

What do we mean by the term *canon*? *Canon* (from the Greek *kanon*) means *a standard by which something is measured*. Designating a carpenter's rule, the word was possibly borrowed from a Hebrew term (*qaneh*) referring to a measuring reed six cubits long. Thus, we refer to Scripture as canonical, meaning that it serves as a rule, a measure, or a standard for God's people.

We must not think that the church determined or defined the books in the church's canon. In reality, the church did not create the canon but received the canon that God created for His people. The church recognized the canonical books as spiritually superlative writings by which all other books were measured and found to be of secondary value in general church use.[4]

The Old Testament Canon

Most of the Old Testament canon, especially the Law and the Prophets, was established long before the time of Christ. The details of the process by which the Old Testament writings were recognized as authoritative and distinguished from other Jewish works remain largely unknown.

Later, Judaism believed that the Word of God came in 24 books. The Talmudic treatise *Baba Bathra* (ca. A.D. 200) contains a list of books virtually the same as the present canon. The books are listed in tripartite form: the five books of Moses, eight books of the Prophets, and eleven Writings.

Law	Prophets	Writings
Genesis	Joshua	Ruth
Exodus	Judges	Chronicles
Leviticus	Samuel	Ezra
Numbers	Kings	Esther
Deuteronomy	Isaiah	Job
	Jeremiah	Psalms
	Ezekiel	Proverbs
	12 Minor Prophets	Ecclesiastes
		Song of Songs
		Lamentations
		Daniel

It is likely that Jesus and the apostles shared this view of the Old Testament (see Luke 24:44). The implications of Jesus' words in Matthew 23:35 (also see Luke 11:51) are most informative. He speaks of "all the righteous blood shed on the earth ... from the blood of righteous Abel to the blood of Zechariah, son of Berechiah." Abel was obviously the first righteous person to suffer at the hands of the wicked, but why include Zechariah? The reference to Zechariah, son of Jehoiada (see 2 Chronicles 24:20-22), is not chronologically the Old Testament's last martyr. He is mentioned because, probably, by the time of Jesus,

Chronicles was recognized as the last book in the Hebrew Bible.

Josephus, the Jewish historian (ca. A.D. 37-100), followed the tripartite grouping but included only 22 books. The reason is that he included only nine Writings since Judges through Ruth was considered one book, as was Jeremiah through Lamentations. The Dead Sea Scrolls indicate that the Qumran covenant community had commentaries on most Old Testament books. These commentaries point to the high regard the covenanters had for the Scriptures. These writings make clear a marked difference between the canonical Scriptures and the numerous other books in the Qumran library.

Much debate surrounds the details of the recognition of the Old Testament canon. Tradition has it that Ezra was primarily responsible for collecting the material into a recognized canon. Critical scholars challenge this tradition, since they date several Old Testament books after Ezra. They instead point to a council of Jewish elders held at Jamnia (ca. A.D. 90) as the important time for establishing the Old Testament canon. But the supposed role of the Council of Jamnia has been severely attacked by recent scholarship, as have other crucial assumptions of the non-evangelical reconstruction. R.T. Beckwith contends that the closing of the Old Testament canon was settled by the time of Judas Maccabaeus, around 165 B.C.[5] It is probable that the Old Testament canon was settled by the time of Jesus. In the absence of enough evidence on the origin of the Old Testament canon, it is impossible to be certain. As men of old were moved by the Spirit to write the books (see 2 Peter 1:21), God led His people to preserve and treasure these writings.

The New Testament Canon

The New Testament writings functioned authoritatively from their beginning; yet, as with the Old Testament, the collection and distinction from other literature of the time were gradual processes spanning several centuries.

Authority was inherent in Jesus' commission to the apostles (see Matthew 28:18), but it was not accepted without question by all (see 1 Corinthians 9:1-3). Not all books written by apostles were included in the canon (see 1 Corinthians 5:9; Colossians 4:16). But by the late second century Irenaeus considered apostolicity the fundamental test of canonical authenticity. Non-apostolic authors, like Mark, Luke, and James, were considered to have equal authority because of their association with and sanction by the apostles.

When the apostolic writings were initially gathered is not known for sure. By the time of the writing of 2 Peter, several letters of Paul were known (see 2 Peter 3:16). Letters were expensive to produce. Certainly, letters from apostles would have been welcome blessings for the young churches during a time when no official New Testament existed. The churches' leadership was provided by the Spirit's ministry through gifted people (see 1 Corinthians 14; Ephesians 4:11-16). The apostles' letters were to be read in the struggling churches during their worship meetings (see Colossians 4:16). They would have been received as valuable directives. The letters of Paul were widely circulated and read by the beginning of the second century (see 1 Clement 47:1-3).

Tradition has held that the decisive period in the history of the New Testament canon was A.D. 140-200, during which time the basic form of the canon developed. The reason for the canon's fixture came largely as a result of the church's need to counter the heresies of marcionism and montanism. The New Testament canon, in the majority, was completely accepted by the end of the second century.

The Muratorian Fragment, dated about A.D. 200, is viewed as the earliest datable list in the history of the New Testament canon. The text is in Latin but most likely was translated from Greek. The list includes four Gospels, Acts, the 13 Pauline Letters, 1 Peter, 1 John, and the Apocalypse of John. It claimed that the Shepherd of Hermas may be read for devotional purposes but not in church worship. Hippolytus of Rome (ca. A.D. 236) has been widely suggested as the author of the list, but this cannot be proved.[6]

By the fourth century Eusebius, the early church historian, delineated several categories of books: (1) accepted, (2) disputed, (3) rejected, and (4) heretical. The accepted books contain most of our present New Testament books. The disputed group contains James, Jude, 2 Peter, and

2 and 3 John. Revelation was accepted by some and rejected by others.

The first list of canonical books that contains the 27 books currently accepted appears in Bishop Athanasius' festal letter in A.D. 367. The order, however, is different. The first church council to list all 27 books of the New Testament was the Council of Carthage in A.D. 397. The selection of the canonical books stabilized after each book proved its worth by passing the tests of canonicity.[7]

We have referred to these tests, but now we need to pursue this issue in more detail. First, it is important to recognize that most New Testament books were considered canonical prior to the application of any kind of tests. The tests only helped the church recognize what was already true: that these books are inspired and authoritative. Neither the church councils nor the application of these tests made any book authoritative or authentic. The book was inspired, authoritative, and therefore genuine when it was written. The councils recognized and verified certain books as the written Word of God, and eventually those so recognized were collected in what we call the Bible.

The tests involved the following issues:

1. Was the book authored or sanctioned by an apostle or a prophet?
2. Was the book widely circulated?
3. Was the book Christologically centered?
4. Was the book orthodox, that is, faithful to the teaching of the apostles?
5. Did the book give internal evidence of its unique character as inspired and authoritative?

In reality, the early churches displayed surprising unanimity about which books belonged in the inspired collection. Although it is true that a few books, such as Jude and Revelation, were the subjects of considerable debate, no book whose authenticity was doubted by a large number of churches was later accepted. The persecution of the church helped distinguish the canonical books from other helpful writings as the people were forced to decide what books should be protected during times of oppression.

Conclusion

At every point in the transmission, translation, preservation, and canonicity of the Bible we see God's providential hand at work. The testimony of the church witnesses to this providential guidance and cannot readily be dismissed. The 66 books that we have are the Word of God written, inspired, and authoritative. The canon of Scripture is authenticated by the testimony of the Holy Spirit, who inspired the writings, to the individual Christian and to the community as a whole.

When we read our present translations, we can read with the assurance that they faithfully represent the original sources. Also, we believe that they include not more or less than the writings God purposed to include in the canonical Scriptures.

Since God has nowhere provided a table of contents for the Bible, the question arises, How do we know that new books should not be added? While this is a complex question, we believe that the canon is closed and includes the right books. This affirmation is based on the recognition that the church of the second, third, and fourth centuries was much closer to the time of the apostles and thus in a better position to recognize and preserve the written prophetic-apostolic materials. To consider expanding the canon simultaneously underestimates the stability of the canon as it has been held by the church during the past 15 centuries and overestimates the creativity of the post-Reformation period. Our belief in a closed canon also grows from a confidence that God in His providence not only inspired authors of Scripture to write those things He wanted to communicate to His people but also superintended their collection and preservation. These issues direct us to another important question: How is this canonical Scripture to be employed and interpreted? The next chapter will concentrate on this question.

Endnotes

[1] F.F. Bruce, *The New Testament Documents: Are They Reliable?* (Downers Grove: InterVarsity Press, 1960), 16-17.

[2] Much of the material in these opening sections is from F.F. Bruce, *The Books and the Parchments* (London: Pickering & Inglis, 1963); Bruce M. Metzger, *The Text of the New Testament* (New York: Oxford University Press, Inc., 1968); P.R. Ackroyd and C.F. Evans, eds., *The Cambridge History of the Bible*, vol. 1 (Cambridge: University Press, 1970).

[3] See F.F. Bruce, *The English Bible* (New York: Oxford University Press, Inc., 1970).

[4] See David G. Dunbar, "The Biblical Canon," *Hermeneutics, Authority, and Canon*, ed. D.A. Carson and John D. Woodbridge (Grand Rapids: Zondervan Publishing House, 1986), 299-360.

[5] See R.T. Beckwith, *The Old Testament Canon of the New Testament Church* (Grand Rapids: William B. Eerdmans Publishing Company, 1985).

[6] See Ralph P. Martin, "Muratorian Canon," *New International Dictionary of the Christian Church*, ed. J.D. Douglas (Grand Rapids: Zondervan Publishing House, 1978), 684-85. A revised history of the New Testament canon has been suggested by A.C. Sundberg, Jr., "The Bible Canon and the Christian Doctrine of Inspiration," *Interpretation* 29 (Richmond: Union Theological Seminary, 1925), 352-71. It is based on redating the Muratorian canon in the fourth century instead of the second. Although the theory has received much attention, the evidence for such a revision is extremely thin.

[7] See the expanded discussions in F.F. Bruce, *The Canon of Scripture* (Downers Grove: InterVarsity Press, 1988), and Bruce M. Metzger, *The Canon of the New Testament* (Oxford: University Press, 1987).

CHAPTER 8

The Use and Interpretation of the Bible

Word Alert

Kerygma—a Greek term for the apostolic preaching of the Gospel found in the New Testament. The six basic aspects of this preaching include:

1. Jesus is the fulfillment of the Old Testament messianic promises.
2. This fulfillment has taken place through the ministry, death, burial, and resurrection of Jesus Christ.
3. By virtue of the resurrection, Jesus has been exalted to the right hand of God.
4. The presence of the Holy Spirit in the church is a sign of Christ's present power and glory.
5. This messianic age will reach its consummation at the return of Christ.
6. A call to repentance issues in the forgiveness of sins and the gifts of the Holy Spirit.

Apostolic fathers—a group of early Christian writers believed to have had direct contact at one time with the apostles of the church. The term is used to describe the earliest noncanonical writings of the late first and early second centuries.

Allegorical interpretation—a kind of biblical interpretation assuming that the text to be interpreted intends to say something other than what its literal wording suggests. This

---

approach seeks to draw out the deeper, mystical sense of a passage of Scripture.

Tropological interpretation—a type of biblical interpretation that attempts to discover the moral sense behind the literal meaning of a Scripture passage.

Anagogical interpretation—a method of biblical interpretation that seeks to unfold the spiritual meaning of a Scripture passage as it relates to eternal or future realities.

Christological interpretation—an approach to biblical interpretation that seeks to see Jesus Christ as central to all interpretation of the Old Testament.

Typological interpretation—an approach to biblical interpretation in which persons, events, or things of the Old Testament are interpreted as foreshadowings of persons, events, or things in the New Testament. Typological interpretation differs from an allegorical one in that the latter sees the hidden meaning of a text, whereas the former understands a revelatory connection between two historically distinct but spiritually significant persons or events.

Functional/pietistic approach—an approach to biblical interpretation that reads the text with an emphasis on the contemporary spiritual significance of the passage rather than on the historical meaning.

Historical-critical models—a term used broadly to describe all methodologies related to the study of biblical texts. It emphasizes historical, philological, and archaeological analysis of the biblical texts to discover the historical setting of a document, such as the time, place, and sources behind the text.

Sensus plenior—a Latin term indicating that God intended a fuller meaning of a passage of Scripture, although it was not clearly understood by the human author or by the original hearers/readers.

Normative meaning—an expression suggesting that the interpreters' findings have authority for the contemporary interpreters of Scripture and may even be binding on the interpreters.

Literal interpretation—an attempt to understand Scripture in its plain and ordinary sense without seeing a deeper or spiritual meaning.

Exegesis—broadly speaking, to explain the meaning of a text in its original context.

The church has used the Bible in a variety of ways. Because of the multifaceted character of the Bible, its use and interpretation have taken a variety of forms. In this chapter we will briefly examine these uses; principles of interpretation, including the Bible's interpretation of itself; and the history of interpretation in the history of the church. Also, this chapter will deal with some contemporary models of interpretation. Finally, the possibility of multiple levels of meaning, or plenary senses, will be addressed.

Biblical Interpretation: The New Testament Pattern

In chapter 2 we briefly looked at Jesus' use of the Old Testament, discovering that Jesus adopted a Christological understanding of the Old Testament. Let us turn our investigation to the writers of the New Testament to see whether that pattern continued.

Following the current rabbinic practices, the apostles employed various approaches to the Old Testament. Moral injunctions were generally interpreted literally. Other Old Testament passages took on an obvious Christological reference, primarily through the use of typological interpretations. Yet no single image or pattern, no one motif of theme adequately expresses the apostles' interpretation of the Old Testament. The New Testament emphasized that numerous themes, images, and motifs of revelation and response are fulfilled in Jesus Christ. The note of Philip's jubilant words "We have found him" (John 1:45, KJV) was echoed by the New Testament writers as the way to interpret the Old Testament events, pictures, and ideas. It was not so much one fulfillment idea but a harmony of notes presented in a variety of ways by different methods of interpretation.[1]

Jesus became the direct and primary source for the church's understanding of the Old Testament. The apostles, probably subconsciously rather than intentionally, practiced the procedures of interpretation followed by later Judaism. The Jewish context, however, in which the New Testament was born was not the primary aspect for the formation of Christian interpretation. At the heart of their interpretation a Christocentric perspective can be found. What was needed was a perspective that could transform the Torah (the law of Moses) into the messianic Torah. Through the pattern that Jesus had set and through His exalted lordship expressed through the Holy Spirit, Jesus served as the ongoing source of the early church's approach to the Scriptures.[2]

Biblical Interpretation: Uses of the Bible

From the earliest days of Christian history individual Christians and the church have used the Bible in various ways. This rich heritage influences today's Christians in the ways they use the Bible for individual and corporate purposes. A survey of these uses of Scripture will help us understand the inestimable value of the Word of God.

The Bible and Worship

We do not know for certain what procedure the earliest churches adopted to include Bible reading as a regular feature of worship. But it is certain that the first and primary use of the Bible was in the church's worship. It is imperative to remember that biblical interpretation was grounded in the church's use and understanding of the sacred text, not in the theoretical analysis of scholars. Following the pattern established in the Jewish synagogue, the exposition of the Word was of utmost importance in the church's worship. This pattern started with Jesus' exposition of Isaiah 61 at the beginning of His ministry, which He interpreted in light of His own messianic mission (see Luke 4:16-22), and was continually practiced in the early church's worship (see Acts 13:14-44; 14:1; 17:1; 19:8).

In 1 Timothy 4:13 young Timothy was exhorted to devote attention to the public reading of Scripture. Private study of Scripture was encouraged in 2 Timothy 2:15. The matter of the public reading of Scripture, which was given by the inspiration of God, was able to make the hearer wise unto salvation, which is in Jesus Christ. For this reason, the place of the reading and exposition of Scripture held in public worship was always central. The model Christian service, like the worship in the synagogue, was a Word-of-God service. The reference in 1 Timothy is the first historical allusion to the use of the Scriptures in the church's worship.

The New Testament Letters were read in the public meeting of the churches (see Colossians 4:16; Revelation 1:3). Apparently, the apostles expected their letters to be accepted as authoritative in their own lifetimes (see 2 Thessalonians 2:15; 2 Peter 3:15-16). The letters, as noted before, were gradually accepted, circulated, and read aloud in public gatherings. In this way they became the objects of study and meditation.

The reading of Scripture was accompanied by its exposition. Almost all of the church's interpretation of Scripture and corresponding theologizing developed from the sermon. The real meaning of preaching was set forth by the apostle Paul in 1 Corinthians 1:17-23. He claimed that he came to preach the Gospel, which he identified as the message of the cross, Christ crucified. This preaching was to demonstrate the Spirit's power so that faith would demonstrate God's power (see 1 Corinthians 2:1-6). The apostle's theology of preaching was built on the elements of the *kerygma*: the incarnation, death, burial, resurrection, and ascension of Christ.[3] In this sense, preaching in the context of the worshiping community reenacted the event of Christ, the event that provided shape and meaning not only to worship but also to the lives of the worshipers.

The church's preaching interpreted the Old Testament Scripture in terms of Christ's coming, as evidenced in the church's attitude toward the Old Testament. The church regarded the Law and the Prophets, as well as the events and worship of Israel, as part of the Christian tradition because it believed that they testified of Jesus Christ. For example, in 1 Corinthians 15:3-4 Paul insisted that everything concerning Christ took place "in accordance with the Scriptures." Soon a typological interpretation of the Old Testament became a standard way of expounding the Scriptures in the church's worship. Thus, through the early church's preaching the initial typological exegesis was practiced.[4]

The preaching of the early church was not a dispassionate recital of historical facts, a sort of nondescript presentation of certain truths, interesting enough but morally neutral. No, the facts were meant to become factors in the lives of the worshipers; hence, the constant offer of repentance, pardon, and a place in the new age inaugurated the coming of God's Son.

The church was given the gifts of pastors and teachers so that the community of faith could be built up through reading, preaching, and teaching Holy Scripture to the measure of the stature of Christ in His fullness (see Ephesians 4:11-16; Colossians 1:28). The early church heavily emphasized that Christians are to be instructed in the Scriptures (see Hebrews 5:11-14) and that Christian leaders are to remain faithful to the tasks of interpreting and expounding the Bible (see Colossians 3:16-17; 1 Peter 4:10-11). Thus, as in the synagogue, the church's worship was a Word-of-God worship, grounded in Holy Scripture. This set the pattern for the church's use of Scripture throughout the ages.

The Bible and Private Study

Because copies of the Bible were so expensive to produce in the time of the early church, most copies were owned by communities, not by individuals. Because common people could not possess their own Scriptures, they depended on public readings. Not until after the eighth century A.D. was a smaller and more affordable copy of the Bible available to a large number of people. From this time on, it was possible for wealthy individuals to purchase copies of the Bible and to provide them for others. However, many individuals were illiterate and thus prohibited from private reading.

With the invention of the printing press and the development of the doctrine of the priesthood of believers in the Reformation, the private reading of Scripture increased. The practice of private study had been encouraged since Jerome (A.D. 341-420) and Augustine (A.D. 354-430), but the emphasis on believers' reading and interpreting Scripture is one of the mainstays of post-Reformation Protestantism. The strongest renewal movements have stressed the supreme importance of the devotional use of the Bible.

The Bible and Theology

In the early church theological construction was vitally related to, if not inseparable from, biblical interpretation. The basis of all true biblical theology in the history of the church is a sound exegetical understanding of Scripture. Most, if not all, theological deviations are caused by the neglect of biblical truth or by a faulty interpretation of biblical texts.

The Bible as Literature

Although the Bible was never intended to be read solely as literature, it has undeniable literary qualities and has undoubtedly greatly influenced other literature, particularly in the English-speaking world. From a literary point of view, the Bible contains drama, poetry, narrative, and prose. The intimacy of the Letters has also exerted broad appeal. The Bible is worthy of literary study. This usage has increased greatly in the past decades. Yet the literary study of the Bible is not the reason that it is the best-selling and most frequently read Book in the world.

Biblical Interpretation: A Look at History

From the beginning of the church a dual heritage developed: (1) one that maintains that Scripture's meaning is found only in its primary historical sense and (2) another that considers Scripture's ultimate meaning to rest in its plenary, or full, sense. From these distinctions several models and combinations of models developed for interpreting Scripture in the early church.

The apostolic fathers in the second century found the true understanding of the Bible in the teachings of the apostles. The rise of false teachings (particularly gnosticism) and challenges to accepted orthodoxy created confusion in interpretation. To demonstrate the unity of Scripture and its message, theological frameworks were implemented by such scholars as Irenaeus (ca. A.D. 140-202) and Tertullian (ca. A.D. 155-255). These frameworks served as guides for faith in the church. Continuing the Christological emphasis of the first century, the rule of faith outlined the theological beliefs that found their focus in the incarnate Lord. Sometimes, however, the interpretation of Scripture through this theological grid forced the biblical text into a preconceived set of theological convictions. This approach resulted in a safeguard for the church's message but reduced the possibility of creativity among the individual interpreters. It also tended to divorce the biblical text from its literary or historical context.[5]

Creative biblical interpretation reached new levels with the rise of the school of Alexandria in the third century. The innovation of allegorical interpretation developed in this context. Allegorical interpretation assumes that the Bible intends to say something more than what its literal wording suggests. It seeks to draw out the deeper, mystical sense beyond the words themselves. The two great representatives of the Alexandrian school were Clement (ca. A.D. 150-215) and Origen (A.D. 185-254).

Those in this tradition understood biblical interpretation as a state of ecstatic possession. Therefore, it was appropriate that the biblical words imparted in this way should be interpreted mystically if their inner significance was to be made known. They affirmed the importance of the literal sense of Scripture. The literal sense, however, was not the primary meaning of Scripture. Origen particularly thought it absurd that a God-inspired Bible could not be interpreted spiritually. From this supposition followed Origen's threefold hermeneutical approach. He maintained that the Bible had three different yet complementary meanings: (1) a literal or a physical sense, (2) an allegorical or a spiritual sense, and (3) a tropological or a moral sense. Yet at places the Alexandrians ignored the literal sense and found numerous spiritual meanings in a single passage, thus creating an entire scale of allegorical interpretation.[6] Alexandrian interpretation was primarily practical. The work of these interpreters cannot be understood until this is realized.

The successors of Origen were challenged by the school of Antioch, which emphasized a literal and historical interpretation. The great Antiochene interpreters included John Chrysostom (ca. A.D. 347-407) and Theodore of Mopsuestia (ca. A.D. 350-428). They thought of biblical inspiration as a divinely given quickening of the writers' awareness and understanding, in which their individuality was not impaired and their intellectual activity remained under conscious control. The Antiochenes focused on the biblical writers' aims, motivations, usages, and methods. They believed that the literal-historical sense of Scripture was primary and that from it moral applications were made.[7] The mature exegesis of Theodore and Chrysostom, while literal, was not a crude or wooden literalism that failed to recognize figures of speech in the biblical text. In continuity with the previous practices of Jesus and the early church, the Antiochenes read Scripture Christologically through the application of typological exegesis.

As the church moved into the fifth century, an eclectic and multifaceted approach to interpretation developed, which sometimes emphasized the literal and historical and sometimes the allegorical but always the theological. Augustine and Jerome established the directions for this period. The biblical text was interpreted in its larger context, understood as the biblical canon. The biblical canon established parameters for validating both typological and allegorical interpretations so that the historical meaning remained primary, even though the deeper spiritual meaning was not ignored. Neither the allegorical practices of Alexandria nor the historical emphases of Antioch dominated. A balance emerged, influenced by pastoral and theological concerns. The Bible was viewed from the standpoint of faith, producing interpretations that emphasized the edification of the church, the love of neighbor, and primarily a knowledge of and love for God.[8]

From the time of Augustine the church, following the lead of John Cassian (died ca. 433), subscribed to a theory of the fourfold sense of Scripture: (1) The literal sense of Scripture could, and usually did, nurture the virtues of faith, hope, and love. When it did not, the interpreter could appeal to three additional virtues, each sense corresponding to one of the virtues. (2) The allegorical sense referred to the church and its faith, what it was to believe. (3) The tropological or moral sense referred to individuals and what they should do, corresponding to love. (4) The anagogical sense pointed to the church's expectation, corresponding to hope. For example, the city of Jerusalem, in all its appearances in Scripture, was understood literally as a Jewish city, allegorically as the church of Jesus Christ, tropologically as the souls of men and women, and anagogically as the heavenly city. The fourfold sense characterized interpretation in the Middle Ages.[9]

Martin Luther (1483-1546), the great reformer, began by using the allegorical method but later claimed to have abandoned it. It was Erasmus (1466-1536), more than Luther, who rediscovered the priority of the literal sense. John Calvin (1509-1564), the most consistent interpreter of the Reformation, developed the emphasis on the grammatical-historical method as the foundation for developing the spiritual message from the Bible. Luther's stress on a fuller sense located in the Christological meaning of Scripture linked the reformers with Jesus, the apostles, and the early church.[10]

It is commonly believed that the followers of the reformers shrank from the freedom in interpretation employed by Luther and Calvin. While this is an overstatement and an oversimplification, it is true that they conducted their exposition along new theological boundaries, establishing a new Protestant scholasticism.[11] This new form of scholasticism resulted in an authoritative and dogmatic interpretation. Almost simultaneously, enlightenment thought began to develop. This movement rejected both authoritative and dogmatic approaches, resulting in two reactions: (1) a newfound pietism of Philipp Jakob Spencer (1635-1705) and of August Herman Franke (1663-1727) and (2) a historical-critical method that stressed the importance of the historical over the theological interpretation of the Bible, pioneered by Johann Semler (1725-1791) and Johann David Michaelis (1717-1791). The modern period has continued in one of these directions: the Reformation, pietistic, or historical-critical approach.

Biblical Interpretation: A Contemporary Model

These different models are presented in contemporary Baptist life. The result of our survey indicates the wide variety of interpretations offered by these diverse perspectives. The functional/pietistic approach is common among all who read the Bible devotionally but are not really concerned with interpretation or historical-theological questions beyond moral responses. Reformation and post-Reformation perspectives attempt to interpret Scripture in a confessional setting. Its strengths are its attempt to understand the Bible in its historical context, its faith presuppositions, and the establishment of theological parameters to guard against what the church perceives as heresy. The historical-critical model encourages creativity, as well as intellectual and academic pursuits.

We can adopt strengths from each of these models and can offer the possibility of multiple meanings in the biblical text. We can suggest the real possibility that the entire biblical text in its canonical context contains a surplus of meaning that is not unlike what has traditionally been called *sensus plenior*. This term indicates a fuller meaning in the Scripture than what was possibly intended or known by the author. The more significant the text, the more this is the case.

To illustrate, let us use the example of the word *seed* as it is used in Scripture. The seed promised to Abraham and Sarah (see Genesis 12-22) had an objective, normative meaning to them, the original historical hearers. It meant that God had promised to give them a son. That interpretation can be validated, but the meaning of *seed* is more in-depth. Its use in Genesis 12 with Abraham and Sarah is a resignification of the promise about the seed in Genesis 3:15, in which Eve was promised a seed. Historically, *seed* referred to the immediate children born to Eve and Sarah. But beyond that, *seed* is given a broader canonical meaning in the Davidic covenant in 2 Samuel 7, in which David is promised that his seed would sit on the throne of Israel forever.

In Galatians 3:16-29 Paul illuminated the theological depth of *seed* by showing that its fullest meaning is found in the Lord Jesus Christ. It is very unlikely that the original historical figures, the biblical authors, or the original readers understood *seed* in Genesis 3; 12; or 2 Samuel 7 to refer to Jesus Christ. Yet from a canonical perspective we see that the meaning of *seed* goes beyond, but does not ignore, the meaning understood by the original readers. Eve had a son, as did Sarah. David's son, Solomon, and his sons, as well, sat on the throne referred to in 2 Samuel 7. The full meaning of each of these examples points to Jesus Christ. Because of its canonical shape and divine nature, the biblical text may have a surplus of meaning or a full depth of meaning, which by its very nature can never be exhausted. It is thus possible, though not always the case, that the meaning of a text may actually exceed the conscious intention of the original authors or the understanding of the original readers.

How can these fuller meanings be determined? What parameters exist to limit fanciful excesses? The parameters are located in the text itself and the biblical canon. The fuller meanings must be consistent with the canonical message. Some guidelines will prove helpful as we seek to develop a contemporary model. These include the following:

1. Approach the text with right presuppositions, identified as biblical faith, accepting the Bible as truthful and authoritative.
2. Recognize that the historical and literal meaning of the Bible is the primary meaning but not the limit of meaning.
3. Acknowledge the possibility of a deeper meaning in the

prophetic-apostolic witness.

4. Affirm the human authorship of the text, as well as its divine origin.

5. See the biblical text, more than the author's mind, as the place where meaning is concentrated.

6. Understand that a text rests in its canonical context.

7. View Scripture as a commentary on Scripture, thus affirming the analogy of faith (the practice of comparing Scripture's clear teaching with sections that are less clear) and the *sensus plenior* (the fuller meaning) of Scripture.

8. Expect illumination from the Holy Spirit to assist in interpretation.

9. Expect the Bible to speak to the reader's contemporary concerns.

10. Interpret the Bible in light of the centrality of Jesus Christ.

Conclusion

We believe that the biblical author's meaning is the objective meaning of the Bible and that the interpreter can determine it through dedicated effort to reach back and read the biblical text in its original context and setting. But because it is a canonical Word for the community of believers, the Bible can also be read by and for the present members of the church. We need to maintain both horizons: that of the biblical writer and that of the contemporary interpreter. This effort also helps to restore the Bible to its rightful place in the church. The Bible does not become captive to a select group of scholars but is a Book for the believing community, interpreted by the members of the community. The scholarly community must again find its place in the church as a servant and enabling arm for the rest of the community of the faithful. Biblical interpretation, as well as theological construction in general, can again be seen not only as an academic exercise but also as an exercise for building up the church.

This proposal is not intended in any way as an anti-intellectual or anti-academic approach. However, it places the church's academic community in a servant role for the good of the church. It simultaneously affirms the church's confessional parameters, the illuminating work of the Holy Spirit, and the Baptist belief that all Christians have the privilege and responsibility to read and interpret the Bible for themselves. It is our hope that these guidelines can provide a helpful balance in Baptist life as we wrestle not only with the nature of Scripture but also with the interpretation of the biblical text. Our concerns focus on the historical horizon, as well as on our contemporary setting, as we seek to live under the authority of God's Word. It is the issue of biblical authority on which we will now focus our attention.

Endnotes

[1] See F.F. Bruce, *New Testament Development of Old Testament Themes* (Grand Rapids: William B. Eerdmans Publishing Co., 1969), 12-21.

[2] See C.F.D. Moule, *The Birth of the New Testament* (London: A. & C. Black, 1962), 58-59.

[3] See C.H. Dodd, *The Apostolic Preaching and Its Development* (London: Hodder and Stoughton, 1963), and R.H. Mounce, *The Essential Nature of New Testament Preaching* (Grand Rapids: William B. Eerdmans Publishing Co., 1960).

[4] Most of the material in this section is based on Ralph P. Martin, *Worship in the Early Church* (Grand Rapids: William B. Eerdmans Publishing Co., 1974) 53-76, and on Robert E. Webber, *Common Roots* (Grand Rapids: Zondervan Publishing House, 1978).

[5] See Robert M. Grant and David Tracy, *A Short History of the Interpretation of the Bible* (Philadelphia: Fortress Press, 1984), 73-82.

[6] See Joseph W. Trigg, *Origen: The Bible and Philosophy in the Third-Century Church* (Atlanta: John Knox, 1983), 87-129.

[7] See J.N.D. Kelly, *Early Christian Doctrines*, rev. ed. (San Francisco: Harper and Row, Publishers, Inc., 1978), 75-82.

[8] See Gerald Bonner, "Augustine as Biblical Scholar," *Cambridge History of*

the Bible, 3 vols. (Cambridge: University Press, 1963-1970), 1:541-63.

[9]See Beryl Smalley, *Study of the Bible in the Middle Ages* (Oxford: Blackwell, 1952).

[10]See A. Skevington Wood, *Captive to the Word: Martin Luther's Doctrine of Sacred Scripture* (Grand Rapids: William B. Eerdmans Publishing Co., 1969).

[11]See J.K.S. Reid, *The Authority of the Scriptures: A Study of Reformation and Post-Reformation Understanding of the Bible* (New York: Harper and Row, Publishers, Inc., 1957).

CHAPTER 9

The Authority of the Bible

The ultimate concern in a discussion of the Bible is its authority. This chapter will treat the authority of the Bible and its rightful role to command obedience. The Bible's authority in contemporary challenges, as well as in ethics and decision making, will be noted. The importance of personal and corporate application will conclude the discussion.

Biblical Authority: Its Source

A view of the Bible that affirms its divine inspiration and total truthfulness is of little value if it is not accompanied by an enthusiastic commitment to the Bible's complete and absolute authority. An approach to the subject of biblical authority must begin with God Himself, for in God all authority is finally located. God is His own authority. There is nothing outside Him on which His authority is established. When God made His promise to Abraham, He pledged His own name because nothing or no one was greater by whom He could swear (see Hebrews 6:13). God's authority is the authority of who and what God is. As we learned in chapter 1, who God is has been made known in His self-manifestation, since God can be known only in His self-revelation. The key to God's authority is His revelation. In this manner, revelation and authority are seen as two sides of the same reality. God thus declares His authority in His revelation, and He alone is the ultimate source of authority for all other lesser authorities.

Authority is the right or power to command obedience or belief. God's sovereign, universal, and eternal reign over the entire universe evidences His authority (see Exodus 15:18; Job 26:12; Isaiah 50:2). He establishes His purposes in time and does all things according to His will (see Daniel 4:34-35; Ephesians 1:11). All authority on earth and in heaven comes from God alone. His providential direction over the events of history demonstrates His authority.

Men and women are creatures of the self-revealing, eternal God. Since He has created humankind, life's meaning is found in dependence on and relationship with Him. God exercises authority over His creation; and God's people respond to His authority in obedience and worship, as well as in confession and repentance. God's authority is communicated in the church and its tradition, in human reason, in conscience and experience, in nature and history, in Christ and the Bible. Of course, as noted in chapters 1 and 2, God has ultimately revealed Himself in the person of Jesus Christ (see John 1:1-18; Hebrews 1:1-3). God reveals Himself in all of the ways mentioned above; yet the Bible is the primary means of God's authoritative self-disclosure for people today.

The Bible pictures Jesus' authority in terms of acting for God the Father. Jesus exercises all the rightful authority of God. He forgives sin (see Mark 2:5-8), casts out demons (see Mark 1:27), teaches with authority (see Matthew 5:21-48; 7:28-29), and raises the dead (see Luke 7:11-17; John 11:38-44). As the obedient Son of God, He follows the word of God revealed in the Scriptures and acknowledges and appeals to the Scriptures' authority (see Matthew 4:1-11; John 10:33-36). Jesus' death and resurrection provided victory over sin, evil, and death (see Colossians 2:15; 1 John 3:8). Thus, all authority in heaven and on earth has been given to Him (see Matthew 28:18-20).

Jesus' authority is exercised over the church (see Ephesians 1:20-23) and is uniquely expressed through His personal ambassadors, the apostles (see Mark 3:14; John 17:18; Acts 1:1-8; 2 Corinthians 5:20; Galatians 1:1-2:9). In this way the apostles serve as the foundation of the church (see Ephesians 2:20-3:5). In fulfillment of Christ's promises (see John 14:26; 16:13) the apostles' authority has been placed permanently in their writings. Thus, the Spirit of God has inspired the prophetic-apostolic writings, and the Scriptures become the recognized authority to communicate God's truth, which is to be taught, believed, and obeyed. The Bible, then, is the Book of God's truth. Because the Bible is completely truthful, it must be wholly trustworthy in its affirmations. Because it is truthful and trustworthy, it is our final authority in all things that pertain to life and godliness.[1]

Biblical Authority: Guidelines for Interpretation

We must recognize that God's truth is revealed not through our human capacities but through the Holy Spirit's illumination (see 1 Corinthians 2:6-16). Jesus claimed: "If you continue in my word, you really are my disciples. You will know the truth, and the truth will set you free" (John 8:31-32).

To live in accord with the truth of Scripture and obey its authority, it is necessary to handle the Word of God correctly (see 2 Timothy 2:15). Care must be taken to interpret the Scriptures faithfully. Beyond what we learned in the previous chapter, we can suggest some practical guidelines:

1. We must be careful not to interpret the Scriptures by our experiences or cultural norms, though, of course, we cannot deny our experiential or cultural presuppositions. Instead, we need to interpret our experience and culture by the Bible. If we allow the Scriptures to be interpreted by our experience, our experience will become the higher authority.

2. We must be cautious, not dogmatic, in our interpretations where the Scriptures are not conclusive. Often we are guilty of saying more than the Bible says in such areas as dress, appearance, or cultural practices (see Romans 14; 1 Corinthians 8:10-13). Where the Bible speaks, we should speak; where it is silent, we must take care that our response is consistent with the general teachings in Scripture.

3. We must avoid rationalizing the Bible so as to undercut its authority. Although Scripture is time- and culture-related, we must be cautious before dismissing a scriptural teaching as culture-bound. Anytime we allow current

philosophical or scientific theories to become the standard by which Scripture is interpreted, we may fall into the trap of usurping Scripture's authority.

4. At the same time, we must recognize that we are separated from the prophets and apostles by time and culture. Meanings of words and practices change from generation to generation. We should carefully seek to determine whether a passage is figurative rather than literal. Recent examples from our own culture may prove helpful. Not long ago if something was said to be cool, it meant that it was cold in temperature. Now something said to be cool is considered good or enjoyable. The same can be said for the word *hot*. It is also possible that a word can take on an opposite meaning. A previous generation described an event as bad when it was distasteful. The present generation describes something very good as very bad. So the use of *lion* in 1 Peter 5:8 can refer to Satan, and it can refer to Christ in Revelation 5:5. Paul exhorted the Philippian church to beware of the "dogs" (Philippians 3:2). He does not mean a pack of angry animals but a group of false teachers. These examples point to Bible students' need to take word usage and cultural practices into account when interpreting Scripture.

5. In the previous chapter we suggested that Scripture can possibly have a fuller (plenary) meaning beyond its literal meaning. Yet in our attempt to find the spiritual truths in a passage, we must not read a spiritual meaning into a passage. Fuller meanings must always be extensions of the primary historical meaning and consistent with the Bible's canonical or overall message. A good general principle is to attempt to interpret the Bible in light of its primary historical meaning. This meaning is found by diligently examining the context of a passage, the customs of the time, and the meanings of words and phrases. Only

when we understand Scripture's meaning can we rightly live under its authority.

6. We need to remember that the purpose of biblical interpretation is to bring about Christlikeness in our lives so we will be equipped for service in Christ's church (see 2 Timothy 3:17). Biblical authority means putting God's Word into practice (see Psalm 119:59-60). We must not limit biblical interpretation to one particular method or technique, but we must employ every legitimate means to understand the Bible's message. The benefit of interpretation is hearing and obeying the Word of God—receiving what the Lord says and prayerfully putting it into practice. Biblical authority begins with a willing acceptance of truth. A right response to scriptural authority is characterized by truth, obedience, praise, and thanksgiving.[2]

Biblical Authority: Contemporary Challenges

Challenges to biblical authority often arise when we apply biblical teachings to our modern context. The question we bring to the Bible shifts from, *What did the Scriptures mean to those to whom it was first given?* to, *What do the Scriptures mean to us?* The biblical context and our context are sometimes embedded in different cultures and worldviews. I. Howard Marshall asks, "How is meaning found when what is common sense in one culture is not common sense in another?" Paul's command to obey one's master in all things (Colossians 3:22-23) is addressed to a culture of involuntary slavery. Our economic system differs greatly from that world. Today employees are often partners in their work with employers. Does this kind of relationship call for loyalty or obedience? If we say that for today the biblical command means that we should appropriate respect and loyalty to employers rather than unconditional obedience, are we diluting it or expressing the essential meaning in terms appropriate for contemporary working conditions?[3] Cultural differences challenge us to hear God's Word clearly.

A missionary has related an account of telling the Joseph story (see Genesis 37-50) to a group of Europeans and to a group of Third World people. The Europeans heard the story of Joseph as a man who remained faithful to God no matter what happened to him. The Third World group, on the other hand, pointed to Joseph as a man who, no matter how far he traveled, never forgot his family. Different cultural backgrounds prompted each response. Can we say that one is more consistent with the authority of the biblical story? Is the other one incorrect? Is it possible that both are legitimate understandings?[4] How can an ancient text speak to us authoritatively so that our own cultural, temporal, and social meanings do not become dominant over the historical meaning of the Bible? Certainly, D.A. Carson is right when he says, "No human being living in time and speaking any language can ever be entirely culture-free about anything."[5]

In line with our divine-human (Christological) understanding of Scripture, Harvie Conn has suggested six helpful clues on this subject. From the divine perspective he offers three important guidelines:

1. The beginning point is a commitment to Scripture's total truthfulness. The only proper control for our judgments remains the primary historical meaning of the biblical text.
2. The cultural patterns of the biblical time period do not simply provide God with sermon illustrations. That culture becomes the providentially controlled matrix from which His revelation comes to us (for example, Exodus 3:12; Luke 22:19-20). That context is the place from which the history of God's unfolding special revelation has been manifested. From that cultural particularity come the universals that link the faith of the biblical characters to ours.
3. The Holy Spirit, who brought the first horizon of the text into being (see 2 Peter 1:20-21), must open our hearts and illumine our minds to open the biblical text for our world. The Spirit does not become some mechanical or

magical answering service. Nor does the Spirit become an intermediary between God and us; He is God who addresses us.

Conn also provides three helpful insights from the human perspective:

1. A distancing must take place before we can hear the ancient biblical text for our day. This might sound like just the opposite thing we want to accomplish. But many biblical stories (such as the parables of the prodigal son [Luke 15] or the repentant publican [Luke 18]) need to be distanced from our setting so the parables' "punch lines" can be heard.
2. Our presuppositions and worldview must be reshaped by the Bible. Our values and perspectives must become more and more what God wants them to be. Our vantage point must be shaped by creation, the fall, redemption, and consummation. In this sense, our cultural and temporal distinctions can become a help, not a hindrance, to understanding and responding to the biblical message.
3. Holy Scripture is presented in cultural forms that are different from ours. These cultural forms often need to be restated and translated for our day to speak to matters of our day.[6]

We can maintain our confession of biblical authority, recognizing the divine-human aspects of the nature of Scripture and the interpretation of Scripture. The Bible's truth is untainted by either the culture from which it comes to us or the culture to which it goes. The message of Scripture uses various cultures while simultaneously and authoritatively standing in judgment over them.

Biblical Authority: Application to Today's Issues

We have seen that the Bible is authoritative since it is God's Word to men and women. Guidelines for interpretation enable us to hear and respond to God's Word in our cultural settings. Yet we need to ask, How do we apply these guidelines to such contemporary issues as decision making and ethical practices?

We can recognize that some biblical teachings are specific and universal commands that speak directly to people in all cultures. Some general teachings have universal application. Some biblical principles have implicit authority. Finally, some matters can be addressed only by finding biblical guidelines that can be applied to that issue or question. The following examples will help us understand these guidelines:

1. Passages such as prohibitions against stealing (see Exodus 20:15; Ephesians 4:28) are direct teachings that apply to all people in all times.
2. General teachings on love or justice can be applied to various situations in different settings. People in employee-employer relationships, family relationships, or broader societal situations must seek to apply principles of justice and/or love in these settings.
3. Teachings about drunkenness (see Ephesians 5:18) must be obeyed. Applications about abstinence from alcoholic beverages are implied rather than being direct teachings. Thus, the level of authority is different from the previous examples.
4. Some contemporary issues are not addressed specifically in Scripture. Where should we work? What church should we join? We must approach each of these matters by trying to apply biblical principles. The answer to these issues must be dealt with differently by each of us under the Holy Spirit's guidance.[7]

Understanding that various levels of authority are in the Bible helps us understand that a commitment to biblical authority is not out-of-date. The general teachings of Scripture reveal God's will in a variety of ways. The direct, implied, and applied principles of Scripture can cross the temporal, social, linguistic, and cultural barriers. Thus, we can affirm the adequacy, sufficiency, and authority of the Bible for modern men and women. The Bible can speak, at various levels, to challenges and issues we face in our day.

Conclusion: The Supremacy of Scripture

The Bible is to be seen as the ultimate standard of authority for God's people. The Bible derives its authority from the self-revealing and self-authenticating God. The Bible's authority can and does communicate across cultural, geographical, and temporal differences between the biblical world and our setting. Scripture is authoritative as it is rightly and faithfully interpreted in its historical setting. The Holy Spirit illumines our minds and hearts to understand the biblical message. Likewise, the Spirit leads us to recognize the authority of Scripture and to respond and obey its message today.[8]

The Bible calls for an obedience to the authority of God revealed in His Word, not in reaction to authority or in an authoritarian sense but from a true freedom that belongs to the children of God. We must avoid a concept of freedom that loses a sense of oughtness and responsibility. Simultaneously, we must avoid a swing toward authoritarianism so that our commitment to Scripture's authority is misplaced in a church leader or in a societal trend.

Many people confuse a desire to obey Scripture's authority with a personal insecurity that calls for a leader to tell them constantly what to do or think. More troubling is that some leaders encourage this confusion by commingling a commitment to biblical authority with a type of authority associated with certain positions of church leadership. What is needed more than ever is a clear-cut distinction between human and divine authority so that the authority of the Bible is not undercut or lost through a false equation with human structures.

We demonstrate our concern for biblical authority not only by careful biblical interpretation but also by repentance and prayer. A commitment to the complete truthfulness and trustworthiness (inerrancy) of Scripture is important because it is the foundation that establishes the full extent of Scripture's authority.

Living with a Holy Spirit-prompted desire to respond to the message and authority of the Bible brings reproof and correction (see 2 Timothy 3:16), which result in contribution, discipleship, and enablement for worship and service (see 2 Timothy 3:17). It results in training in righteousness that bears on Christian businesspeople and the integrity of their practice. It bears on Christians, who must speak to matters of injustice in society and in the church. Biblical authority addresses families and their commitments to one another. It speaks to preachers and teachers to handle carefully the Word of God (see 2 Timothy 2:15). The authority of the Bible calls on us to recognize God's desire for unity (through variety) in the church (see Ephesians 4:1-16; John 17; 1 Corinthians 12) and the need to love one another (see John 13:34-35), even when we disagree over the interpretation of Scripture itself. Thus, we need a renewed commitment to biblical authority that enables us to relate to one another in love and humility, bringing about true fellowship and community and resulting in not only right doctrine but also right practice before a watching, unbelieving world. We need a renewed commitment to biblical authority that will transform our performance-oriented church meetings into authentic worship and praise, that will turn our church programs into service that is pleasing to God. The Holy Spirit, through the Scriptures, illumines our appreciation of grace and motivates us toward faithful evangelism, social ministry, and worldwide missions.[9]

We confess that God has revealed Himself to us. His revelation has been preserved for us in Holy Scripture by the Holy Spirit's work of inspiration. We confess our belief in the divine inspiration, total truthfulness, and complete authority of the Bible. Even beyond this affirmation, with willing spirits and open minds and hearts, we must dedicate ourselves anew to the authority of Holy Scripture, assured that we can place our complete confidence in God's truthful and reliable Word.

Endnotes

[1] See Bernard Ramm, *The Pattern of Authority* (Grand Rapids: William B. Eerdmans Publishing Company, 1957).

[2] See Oletta Wald, *The Joy of Discovery* (Minneapolis: Bible Banner Press, 1956).

[3] See I. Howard Marshall, *Biblical Inspiration* (Grand Rapids: William B. Eerdmans Publishing Company, 1982), 105.

[4] See Harvie M. Conn, "Normativity, Relevance, and Relativism," *Inerrancy and Hermeneutic*, ed. Harvie M. Conn (Grand Rapids: Baker Books, 1988), 186-89, and Gordon D. Fee and Douglas Stuart, *How to Read the Bible for All Its Worth* (Grand Rapids: Zondervan Publishing House, 1982), 58-60.

[5] D.A. Carson, *Biblical Interpretation and the Church: The Problem of Contextualization* (Nashville: Thomas Nelson Publishers, 1984), 19.

[6] Conn, "Normativity, Relevance, and Relativism," 197-209.

[7] Some of this material has been developed from insights gained from Ebbie C. Smith's discussion of biblical ethics at Southwestern Seminary.

[8] James Leo Garrett, Jr., *Systematic Theology*, vol. 1 (Grand Rapids: William B. Eerdmans Publishing Company, 1990), 181-82.

[9] See Geoffrey W. Bromiley, "Authority," *International Standard Bible Encyclopedia*, ed. Geoffrey W. Bromiley, 4 vols. (Grand Rapids: William B. Eerdmans Publishing Company, 1979) 1:346-71, and D.A. Carson, "Recent Developments in the Doctrine of Scripture," *Hermeneutics, Authority, and Canon*, ed. D.A. Carson and John D. Woodbridge (Grand Rapids: Zondervan Publishing House, 1986), 46-48.

Bibliography

Beale, Gregory K. *The Erosion of Inerrancy in Evangelicalism: Responding to New Challenges to Biblical Authority*. Wheaton: Crossway, 2008.

Bloesch, Donald G. *Holy Scripture: Revelation, Inspiration, and Interpretation*. Downers Grove: InterVarsity, 1994.

Boice, James M., ed. *The Foundation of Biblical Authority*. Grand Rapids: Zondervan, 1978.

Bruce, F.F. *The Canon of Scripture*. Downers Grove: InterVarsity, 1988.

_____. *The New Testament Documents: Are They Reliable?* Downers Grove: InterVarsity, 1960.

Bush, L. Russ and Tom J. Nettles. *Baptists and the Bible – 40th Anniversary Edition*. Fort Worth: Seminary Hill Press, 2020.

Carroll, B.H. *The Inspiration of the Bible*. New York: Revell, reprint 1930.

Carson, D.A. *The Collected Writings of Scripture*. Compiled by Andy Naselli. Wheaton: Crossway, 2010.

_____. *The Enduring Authority of the Christian Scriptures*. Grand Rapids: Eerdmans, 2016.

Carson, D.A. and John D. Woodbridge, eds. *Hermeneutics, Authority, and Canon*. Grand Rapids: Zondervan, 1986.

_____, eds. *Scripture and Truth*. Grand Rapids: Zondervan, 1983.

DelHousaye, John, John J. Hughes, and Jeff T. Purswell, eds. *Scripture and the People of God*. Wheaton: Crossway, 2018.

Dockery, David S. *Christian Scripture: An Evangelical Perspective on Revelation, Inspiration, and Interpretation*. Nashville: B&H, 1995.

_____. "Special Revelation," in A Theology for the Church. Ed., Daniel L. Akin. Nashville: B&H, 2014, 103-54.

Draper, James T. *Trusting Thy Word*. Nashville: Broadman, 1989.

Erickson, Millard J. *Christian Theology*. Grand Rapids: Baker, revised 1998.

Fee, Gordon D. and Douglas Stuart. *How to Read the Bible for All Its Worth*. Grand Rapids: Zondervan, 1982.

Feinberg, John S. *Light in a Dark Place: The Doctrine of Scripture*. Wheaton: Crossway, 2018.

Frame, John M. *The Doctrine of the Word of God*. Phillipsburg: P&R, 2010.

Garrett, James Leo, Jr. *Systematic Theology*. Vol. 1. Grand Rapids: Eerdmans, 1990.

Grudem, Wayne. *Systematic Theology*. Grand Rapids: Zondervan, 1994.

Henry, Carl F.H. *God, Revelation, and Authority*. 6 vols. Waco: Word, 1976-83.

Hodges, Louis Igou. "Scripture," in *New Dimensions in Evangelical Thought*. Ed. David S. Dockery. Downers Grove: InterVarsity, 1998.

Manly, Basil, Jr. *The Bible Doctrine of Inspiration Explained and Vindicated*. New York: Armstrong and Son, 1891.

McAfee, Michael and Lauren Green McAfee. *Not What You Think: Why the Bible Might Be Nothing We Expected Yet Everything We Need*. Grand Rapids: Zondervan, 2019.

Morris, Leon. *I Believe in Revelation*. Grand Rapids: Eerdmans, 1976.

Nicole, Roger R. and J. Ramsey Michaels, eds. *Inerrancy and Common Sense*. Grand Rapids: Baker, 1980.

Packer, J.I. *"Fundamentalism" and the Word of God: Some Evangelical Principles*. Grand Rapids: Eerdmans, 1958.

Poythress, Vern S. *Inerrancy and Worldview: Answering Modern Challenges to the Bible*. Wheaton: Crossway, 2012.

Saucy, Robert L. *Scripture: Its Power, Authority, and Relevance*. Nashville: Word, 2001.

Thompson, Mark D. *A Clear and Present Word: The Clarity of Scripture*. Downers Grove: InterVarsity, 2006.

Trueman, Carl and Paul Helm, eds. *The Trustworthiness of God: Perspectives on the Nature of Scripture*. Grand Rapids: Eerdmans, 2002.

Warfield, B.B. *The Inspiration and Authority of the Bible*. Philadelphia: Presbyterian & Reformed, reprint 1948.

Williams, Peter J. *Can We Trust the Gospels?* Wheaton: Crossway, 2019.

Woodbridge, John D. *Biblical Authority: Infallibility and Inerrancy in the Christian Tradition*. Grand Rapids: Zondervan, revised 2015.